# HOW

# CAN I GET

# THROUGH

# TO YOU

BY D. GLENN FOSTER
& MARY MARSHALL

New York

# BREAKTHROUGH

# HOW

## COMMUNICATION

# CAN I GET

### Beyond Gender,

# THROUGH

### Beyond Therapy,

# TO YOU

### Beyond Deception

Library of Congress Cataloging-in-Publication Data

Foster, D. Glenn.
How can I get through to you? : breakthrough communication—
beyond gender, beyond therapy, beyond deception / by
D. Glenn Foster and Mary Marshall.—1st ed.
p. cm.
ISBN 0-7868-6018-9
1. Typology (Psychology). 2. Interpersonal relations.
3. Personality and situation. 4. Individuality. I. Marshall,
Mary, 1945 Jan. 21– II. Title.
BF698.3F64      1994
158'.2—dc20
93-41883
CIP

Designed by Holly McNeely

FIRST EDITION

10   9   8   7   6   5   4   3   2   1

This is for Hilary and Ian,
and Bill and Whitney

All persons are puzzles until at last
we find in some word or act the key
to the man, to the woman;
straightway all their past words and
actions lie in light before us.

—Emerson, *Journals* (1842)

# CONTENTS

# P R E F A C E

## by Glenn Foster

This is a book about "mind reading."

It is a do-it-yourself guide to understanding that most fundamental of differences between yourself and other people: the distinct ways you think and feel, and how to use those differences to your advantage.

We all expect the people we love to know how to talk to us, how to satisfy our needs, and how to be there for us. They try; with the best will in the world they try, but more often than not they fail. They constantly do things and say things that surprise, frustrate, infuriate, and just plain totally bewilder us. And in turn, we constantly do and say things that surprise, frustrate, infuriate, and just plain totally bewilder them.

They don't understand what we want from them at all, even when we try to tell them. They can't reach us because they don't understand how we think and feel.

And clearly, we don't understand them.

As hard as we try, we both remain separate and alone, unable to make that final connection with each other that we both so desperately need. There seems to be no way of discovering exactly what it is that makes each of us tick, what it is that makes us appear to be wired up differently.

We so often say frivolously, yet with more than a tinge of desperate frustration, "If only I could get inside his head . . . ," or, "If only I knew what was going on in her mind . . . ," then "I'd know who this person *really* is."

*How Can I Get Through to You?* is a practical, systematic, step-by-step guide that answers how to do exactly that.

The germ of this system began over twenty years ago when, as a young polygraph examiner with the Atlanta Police Department, I became convinced that the human eye, ear, and instinct were recorders and analyzers of human deception far superior to any mechanical device.

Over and over again, I found that the stimulation test—the stage leading up to the polygraph examination itself, when you simply talk with and listen to subjects before they are hooked up to all the stress-indicating instruments—told me more about the subjects than the test itself was ever capable of picking up. The very way they expressed themselves, quite apart from what they actually said, offered a tantalizing glimpse into who and what they really were—as opposed to who they wanted me to believe they were.

As a result of this discovery, I began to spend my off-days not studying machines, but sitting in the back of courtrooms with my eyes closed, *listening* to what people said and the way they said it.

Listening to the examination and cross-examination of men and women, old and young, intelligent and stupid, educated and uneducated, inarticulate and highly articulate to the point of being glib, as their voices changed dramatically or barely perceptibly in pitch, volume, speed, and tone, I started listing the variations and noting how their voices appeared to be signaling when they either revealed or hid the truth.

I began noting specifically the ways they used and arranged not only words but silences and sounds in their sentences, and I then cross-referenced my findings with the voice-variation signals.

Patterns emerged. They were patterns that indicated precisely how and when subjects were trying to deceive or hide something from others, or even from themselves.

Both literally and metaphorically, I opened my eyes and began watching these people, looking for additional evidence in the way they moved their bodies, set their faces, or even blinked in concert with the signals they were sending through their voices.

A second tier of patterns emerged, complementary to the first. With the melding of both patterns, the overall picture became very clear. It was a picture that showed how people's voices and bodies invariably give them away when they are lying. Hard as they try, no subjects can control *all* the telltale signals their bodies send out when they are being deceptive. Further, the signals become far more pronounced and obvious when the deceivers are in stress.

As a final proof, the pattern of signals sent out by people who were telling the truth was, in every independently verified case, very different from that telegraphed by a liar.

It seemed to me that a full and complete system of lie detecting was forming from my research. However, observations and theories are of little practical use to the criminal interviewer until they can be proved. For the next five years, I sought out every opportunity to interview people one on one in the world of law enforcement at every level—local, city, county, state, and federal—testing and retesting my findings against the actual behavior of the hundreds of men and women I interviewed. Those theories that did not stand up in practice I discarded; those that did I continued to hone.

Along the way, I developed techniques for recognizing and identifying the voice and body patterns of a liar, for pinpointing the exact area of deception, and for persuading liars to reveal the truth by using their own speech and voice patterns to bond with them and gain their trust.

As a consulting interviewer, my method became more and more successful in getting confessions in difficult cases, and I was approached by law enforcement bodies across the country to teach the techniques I had developed.

For the first time, this forced me actually to correlate and systematically organize both my theoretical research and practical field work, which revealed yet another, even more significant pattern. It was that there are only four quite separate and distinct "styles" that human beings use to communicate, or in the case of liars, *not* to communicate.

These four "styles" of communication that emerged struck me as being remarkably similar to the "personality" types identified by the early twentieth-century psychoanalyst Carl Jung in his pioneering work with abnormal patients. Jung, however, postulated eight fundamental types: four introvert and four extrovert.

My work, by contrast, suggested that in practice, as far as distinct ways of communicating are concerned, there are only four types: one introvert and three extrovert.

Once an interviewer knows which of the four styles of communication a subject uses, by applying the techniques I had developed he or she can "read"—and even predict—a subject's thoughts and emotions so thoroughly, and bond with the subjects so convincingly, that subjects can be persuaded to divulge the truth to someone who they feel—perhaps for the first time in their lives—really understands them.

Over the next few years, while teaching these developing techniques to law enforcement investigators across the United States, Canada, and Mexico, and continuing to interview particularly hard-to-break suspects for federal and state cases, I synthesized these techniques into a complete and systematic method.

This method is a holistic system of understanding and communicating with a human being. In interviewing and working with thousands of men and women *in extremis* in the real
world, I have been in a unique position to observe people
as a whole and to study whether established and newfound
discoveries about human nature and functioning have any
practical relevance in understanding the behavior—mental,
physical, and verbal—of a single human being.

However, when a man or woman's fate and freedom de-
pend on my reading of his or her behavior, there is no place
for the luxury of theory or the niceties of supposition. We
need the inarguable certainty of fact, reality: the unvar-
nished truth.

Nevertheless, I am deeply grateful to the men and women
who have made these discoveries, and have developed and
clinically tested their theories about human perception, emotions, linguistics, and, in recent years especially, about how
the human brain works in physiological terms. I have drawn
freely on their work, but have adapted and developed only
those parts of their diverse theories and discoveries that I
could prove empirically have a bearing on the way human
beings actually communicate with each other in the real
world. Thus, I have been able to systematize an entire "language" of spoken and unspoken, conscious and subconscious
communication.

Aware constantly of the need for practical application, I de-
vised techniques for recognizing, identifying, and using this
"language" for the sole purpose of enabling an interviewer to
*read* a subject and, *responding* directly to the subconscious
language, to maneuver him into a state of such intense rapport that he drops all his defenses and replies directly,
openly—truthfully.

In use, the method proved to be so uncannily successful
that it was adopted not only by the FBI, the Bureau of Alcohol,
Tobacco and Firearms (ATF), and other authorities through-

out the United States, but also by the Royal Canadian Mounted Police and Mexican law enforcement bodies. I found myself teaching it in classes and seminars across the country almost full time.

By this point it was possible for an interviewer to recognize and identify a subject's entire personality and communication profile within the first thirty seconds of meeting, before either the interviewer or the subject had even spoken a single word to each other.

Early in 1991, I believed that the method, with its two principal techniques of *Read* and *Respond,* was as complete and developed a model as possible for its intended application in the arena of high stress, confrontational criminal interview, and interrogation.

Then, at a seminar I held in Charleston, South Carolina, I met Mary Marshall, who added a third arm—that of *Reciprocate*—and catapulted the entire method out of that limited world into another, far wider one.

At the time, she was working in international law. Through a recommendation from a U.S. Attorney who had attended an earlier seminar, Mary—like many other lawyers over the years—had come to my seminar with the sole aim of honing and updating her already considerable interviewing and cross-examining skills.

However, Mary's experience and expertise was not solely in the field of international business law. Earlier, she had spent fifteen years in England and Australia involved in another world: the to her mind depressingly acrimonious world of family and matrimonial law, with all its attendant miseries of failed marriage counseling, pointless "reconciliation" programs, and inadequate "therapy"—all leading inevitably to a vicious melee of restraining orders, property settlements, child custody battles, and, at each stage, unhappiness for everyone involved.

She had come away from that period of her life with a deep

dissatisfaction with so-called just and legal solutions to dete-
riorating personal relationships, an intense contempt for
"quick-fix" pop psychology methods of marital and personal
reconciliation, and a profound distrust for the institution of
marriage counseling. She even had very serious doubts about
the benefits and efficacy of any form of psychological therapy
at all.

Suddenly, Mary Marshall found herself examining the
method from an entirely different perspective—with startling
results.

At the end of the third day's class she bombarded me with
questions. She wanted to know, for instance, what would happen if, instead of remaining rigorously objective and playing
a professional "role" with the subject to extract his secrets,
the interviewer suddenly began to tell the subject something
about herself that was also true and deeply secret?

The reply of course was that no interviewer would volunteer that information.

But what if the subject had the ability to read and respond
to the interviewer, and extract it from him whether or not he
intended to volunteer it?

I informed her that the sort of close intimate bonding that
would produce would be the last thing required in a professional meeting between interviewer and criminal.

She responded that it was not the *last* thing required in
what she could only describe as a desperately amateur clash
between ordinary people fighting blindly and chaotically to
save their relationships; it was the *first* thing—and something
both she and almost everybody else in the world involved in
a relationship, or even merely wanting to be involved in a
relationship, had been looking for for years.

If one person could be taught to use the techniques of *Read*
and *Respond* against another person with such dramatic success, could two people be taught to use the same techniques
*for* each other with equally successful results?

Could the method take another turn—out of the world of criminals and law enforcement into the wider world of ordinary people and relationships and love?

The answer was yes, it could. At least, in theory.

The practice, even before it was systematized into book form by Mary Marshall, took another year and a half to get right.

Naturally, no single idea or system of ideas springs fully formed. It is always the end product of the many earlier, pioneering ideas that have gone before and made it possible.

In our months of discussions and trials, then more discussions and retrials, so many people have given freely not only of their time and interest but often much of the workings of their intimate thoughts, that otherwise would have been kept private and carefully guarded. We are grateful to them for their trust. With their permission, a number of their stories appear pseudonomously as illustrations to important points in the course of the book.

Similarly, we are grateful for the work of all the pioneers in the disparate fields of human relationships and communication this book has drawn on for its final form. To avoid mention of Desmond Morris's two major books on body language—*The Naked Ape* and *Manwatching*—would not only be a discourtesy but an unforgivable omission of work that was both groundbreaking and influential. In the field of general human behavior, the work of Julius Fast, Gerald I. Nierenberg, and Henry H. Calero also influenced the direction of our thinking. Edward T. Hall's books, *The Silent Language* and *The Hidden Dimension*, were important signposts in that direction, as were Ray L. Birdwhistell's theories on Kinesics, and Paul Ekman's work on emotional displays.

The lectures and monographs of Richard O. Arthur and Frank Horvath on truth and deception signals in interview and interrogation situations reminded us both that much of the ground-clearing efforts that made our present work possible began as far back as the 1950s, though it was little noticed or appreciated at the time.

The collected works of Carl Jung served as a foundation for further investigation of the theory of personality types, as did the later developments of that theory by David Keirsey and Marilyn Bates, Katherine Cook Briggs and Isabel Briggs Mysers. Sadly, we found their theories in many instances to be just that—theories—and unworkable in practice; but they served as embarkation points to further research that led us, finally, to discoveries that were workable.

On that journey of discovery, so often John Oldham and Lois Morris's rewriting of the American Psychiatric Association's "bible" of abnormal personality behavior, *DSM-III-R*, in terms of normal personality was a welcome temporary landfall.

Our gratitude for the work of Elisabeth Kübler-Ross in charting the five stages of the terminally ill through Denial, Anger, Bargaining, Depression, and Acceptance cannot be overemphasized. Her work formed the basis for our development of the idea that these are also the five stages that the living go through each day of their lives, and was seminal.

The lectures of Richard Bandler and John Grinder in the field of neurolinguistic programming were also valuable, as was the early work of Frederick C. Link on interview and interrogation technique, set out in his book *The Kinesic Interview Technique* written with Glenn Foster.

Other works and monographs often consulted include John Hocking and Dale Leathers's *Non-Verbal Indications of Deception—A New Theoretical Perspective;* Brent Rubin's *Non-Verbal Behavior and Social Psychology;* and, most recently, Deborah Tannen's two books, *That's Not What I Meant!* and *You Just Don't Understand.*

By design, this book is written not for experts or luminaries in any one field; it is written for ordinary readers in, we hope, plain style.

Extraordinary, however, among the many ordinary readers who first read it in manuscript form and offered suggestions and revisions, or simply the encouragement to keep on with what, at times, seemed a never-ending task, was our New York agent, Jane Gelfman of Gelfman Schneider. We thank her deeply, and—as ever—with love.

# HOW

# CAN I GET

# THROUGH

# TO YOU

# INTRODUCTION

## by Mary Marshall

It is in our very nature as human beings to want to share ourselves. We do not like being alone and separate: we want to share our dreams, hopes, and fears with those who want to share theirs with us. We want to be understood by those we can understand in return.

We want to share our happiness with those who delight in our pleasure, to share our sadness with those who feel our pain, and we want to be as important in other people's lives as they are in ours.

Yet, for all our wanting it, we cannot make it happen. So often we seem unable to make our relationships work at all. Not only do we fail really to understand the people closest to us, we can't even make them understand us. They don't satisfy our needs, they can't feel our pain, they will not share our dreams—and we fail them just as badly.

Yet we all go on trying.

In every relationship, we shy away from people who don't like the way we are, and we are drawn to people who find certain things about us appealing. If people like the way we look, the way we do things and say things, we respond to

3

their interest. Because they find us attractive, we tend to find the way they look, behave, think, and talk interesting in return. There is mutual appeal.

If someone *loves* the way we are—and the feeling is mutual—we both want to share ourselves with each other. We want to let the other person into our lives, tell him or her things about ourselves which are important to us and receive approval, support, and admiration. We want this person to do even more—we want him or her to understand us. And, in return, we want to be able to reciprocate with a deep understanding of everything about this person who loves us.

While we find ourselves attracted to people who have something in common with us, we tend not to be drawn to people who are exactly like us. Our interest and curiosity is aroused by someone with a different approach to life than ours.

A married couple who helped in the research for this book are a perfect example. They both love foreign travel so much each is prepared to live like a pauper for eleven months in order to pay for one month each year in a different country. Yet, although they both anticipate the trip with equal excitement, each of them goes about it in a very different way.

He believes he has to know the history, the customs, the politics of any place before he can even set foot in it, and plans a precise schedule so they know exactly where they'll be and when.

She, on the other hand, does no forward planning, preferring just to arrive and wander where fancy dictates.

Each year for eleven months she complains loud and long about his "petty, bureaucratic" mind, as he complains of her "aging, flower person" mentality. They both know that his tight schedules never work in practice, and that her casual attitude often lands them in trouble; but it doesn't stop either of them, year after year, doggedly sticking to a distinct approach.

Yet each year they return with wonderful stories of their adventures together. Even though he could not leave before doing his precise preparation, he finds her attitude of serendipity strangely appealing. He finds it comforting to know that, when his schedule goes awry, his momentary panic at facing unpredictable and unplanned situations will be soothed by her calm assurance and delight at the opportunity to improvise.

For her part, while she will never be able to bring herself to plan ahead the way he does, she somehow finds the fact that he does so reassuring. It creates, for her, a structured boundary within which she feels secure enough to meander.

Their differences complement each other. They are both reassured and comforted by each other's attitudes. They are supported by each other. It's as if, alone, each is only half prepared for what may happen; but together, they are completely prepared—they are whole. Between them, they have created a world in which they can both move with freedom, dignity, and confidence.

Like these two people who are attracted to each other by their very differences in temperament, we are all susceptible to the sense of comfort and support—of completeness—that someone else's complementary differences offer.

We all find ourselves drawn to people whose reactions to the world are different from ours. We see something in the way they behave that we admire—that we wish we could emulate, but cannot. And they, in turn, frequently feel the same attraction to that very aspect of our behavior which they feel they lack.

For example, the person who is stunned into silence when someone puts him down, who can never think of what he should have said until much later, admires the person who always seems to have a lightning-fast riposte ready. Yet, in truth, the person who can produce that quick retort often feels she is merely blurting out the first overemotional, ill-considered thing that comes into her mind, and she finds herself admiring the person she perceives as being able to control his tongue until he thinks of something more considered and moderate to say.

Similarly, a person who finds it difficult to get along with others, who is shy and withdrawn, often admires someone who seems to radiate an easy charm that has strangers confiding the most intimate details of their lives to her within minutes of first meeting—without realizing that this gregarious person he admires so much may secretly wish she could be as impervious to everyone's problems as the more withdrawn—seemingly aloof—person appears to be.

It is the old adage that "opposites attract" in action.

Similar instances of opposites attracting are many and varied. But in every case, those aspects of one person's temperament that complement other, seemingly missing, aspects of someone else's nature are just that: merely aspects. They are component *parts* of a series of characteristics that form the whole of each person's fully rounded personality.

For example, the man we described earlier who finds himself compelled to make precise travel plans is acting in accordance with a deeply ingrained urge in his personality to control not just his vacation schedule but his entire environment. This need to control even extends to his relationships.

In the same way, the woman whose nature exerts an equally compelling urge for her to wander unrestrained by travel schedules is reacting to the dictates of her personality to live her life in as unfettered and unstructured an environment as possible—an attitude that extends to her relationships as well.

As we saw earlier, in good times, certain aspects of these two people's personalities complement the other's so perfectly that each of them is comforted and reassured by it. Yet, in bad times, *other* aspects of these same two personalities can often jar and grate against the other—and they do. These two people, however, are sustained through the bad times by the mutual respect and admiration that they have nourished in that one month when they believe they see the other person for who he/she really is—and realize how deeply they love what they see.

But certain differences in whole personalities, while they may be admirable and attractive in normal circumstances, when taken to extremes, do more than just grate and jar—they positively repel.

Look again at the person who always has a lightning-fast retort on the tip of her tongue, who is admired by the more considered person. This naturally fast-thinking, quick-talking type is also capable of swift and dramatic mood swings. She can suddenly explode into an anger that stuns and horrifies her slower-thinking admirer. Then, when she can just as suddenly shed that anger, the other person may be left confused, perhaps more than a little frightened, and certainly no longer admiring.

In contrast, the person who thinks and reacts in a slower, more considered way is prone to ponderous mood changes and is so slow to rise to anger it can mystify, confuse, and finally infuriate the one-time admirer. The fact that this anger can be maintained over such a very long period leaves the more mercurial admirer even more perplexed.

When completely at odds, these two people can irritate and exasperate each other beyond measure. Like magnets that attract at one pole and repel at another, these people's differences—instead of being the basis for warmth and comfort—become the triggers to stress, confrontation, and unhappiness.

All of us are painfully aware of the deep unhappiness that arises when we are confused by the way our opposites sometimes behave. We are at a loss to understand *why* they are acting and reacting the way they do. We are totally incapable of dealing with it—we just don't understand.

We don't understand because it bears no relation to the way *we* behave. We are puzzled by someone who suddenly says something we would never dream of saying. We are baffled when someone suddenly does something that we could never see ourselves doing. We try to interpret the meaning of another person's behavior in terms of our own, but it makes no sense—it just seems bizarre. His or her motivations are obviously nothing like ours. Whatever it is that makes the other person tick is certainly not what makes *us* tick. We keep trying to put a finger on just what it is that makes another person so different from us, without success.

And since we don't even know how to begin to understand another person, we wonder if it will ever be possible to get him or her to understand *us*.

The foundation for mutual understanding lies in comprehending those essential differences between one person and another that make us think other people must be wired up quite differently.

The differences between all of us as human beings are rooted in, and spring from, the particular type of personality each of us has, has always had, and always will have. It is this distinct personality type that dictates the way we act and react, not just physically and verbally, but mentally as well. We *think and feel* differently from people whose personalities are different from ours.

While we often suspect that the dissimilarities in the way we think and feel are enormous, we do not realize just how staggeringly large they really are. The way a person with a different personality thinks and feels is not just a minor variation or slight aberration of the way we think and feel, but is as different, unfamiliar, and foreign as English is to Arabic.

The people around us whom we love or hate or are frustrated by are not being different or contrary or petulant out of perversity or malice when they do not seem to want to understand and agree with the way we think and feel: they are incapable of thinking and feeling as we do. *They are not us.*

While we are drawn to some of the features of another's personality that are different from yet complementary to our own, we do not realize just how deeply rooted and all-encompassing the sum total of those differences is. We arrogantly assume that those parts that are different are nothing more than minor shadings, and that at base, deep down, every other person on earth thinks and feels exactly as we do. We naïvely take it for granted that the wellsprings of their personalities must be the same as ours, their motivations identical, and all their actions, statements, and meanings perfectly explicable in terms of our own.

*This is simply not true.*

To illustrate the immense gap in the way different personalities think and feel, we need only look at just one of the emotions we think all humankind shares: anger.

Anger is a universal emotion, which we assume is experienced by everybody in pretty much the same way.

It is not.

Some of us, who have a certain sort of personality, experience anger as an intensely cold, hard, tight emotion of last resort. When we are finally driven to this anger, it is so all-engrossing we have great difficulty extricating ourselves from its hold over us. We find the power this emotion has to undermine our self-control so frightening we will do almost anything to prevent ourselves reaching that point.

Others of us, with another type of personality, perceive anger very differently. We experience it as an immense range and variety of different feelings, which we can swing in and out of rapidly. It is almost as if we *savor* the anger, roll it around on our tongues to experience its different flavors and textures, and then choose a favorite variety to suit the occasion. Often, it is not an emotion of last resort, but merely a way of expressing ourselves dramatically.

When those of us who have this latter type of personality toy with anger in our own innocuous way, we are surprised and confused by the reactions of our opposites. Our opposites—whose sole experience of anger is of an emotion of such painful potency that they could never conceive of it being used so lightly—are just as surprised and confused. Facing what they in their linear way believe can only be real animus, they feel assaulted and wounded. They are stunned. As stunned as we are by their reactions to what we believe to be no more than a demonstration of mild irritation or dramatic emphasis.

So, frequently, opposites like these find themselves caught up in this sort of confused exchange:

"Why are you so angry over something so trivial?"

"I'm not angry—I'm just irritated."

"If you're just *irritated,* why are you shouting and yelling and waving your arms about?"

"Because this is the way I get irritated! Okay?"

"But it's just not that big a thing—I can deal with it for you in no time at all."

"I don't want you to 'deal with it in no time at all'—that's not the point! Why are you getting so upset, anyway? I'm not irritated at *you!*"

"Look, just leave it to me and I'll fix it. That way you can stop worrying about it."

"I'm not *worrying* about it! I'm just irked by it. And I certainly don't need someone else to fix it for me!"

"Whoa! Stop! It's just not that important. I don't understand why you're being so melodramatic and theatrical about all this."

"*Melodramatic and theatrical?* I'm not being melodramatic or theatrical! This is the way normal people react to something like this. Not everybody's as insipid and lifeless as you are!"

They could be talking about nothing more in the real world than a flat tire, a missed appointment, or a minor social gaffe at a dinner party.

From the beginning, each person is confused and bewildered by the other's reaction, and this confusion and bewilderment grows with every word uttered. Neither of them truly understands the other—they are looking at the other's behavior solely in terms of how each would react him- or herself.

Escalating conflicts like this are not uncommon between people with these types of temperaments, and both are left upset and uncomprehending.

If these two people could see *why* each of them is reacting the way he or she does—if they could understand the wellsprings of the other's differences in temperament and be able to recognize the predictable patterns of action and reaction for that particular personality—their approach would be very different. One would know exactly what makes the other tick, and the other would know exactly where the first is coming from. They would know what to say to each other, and how and when to say it. Their ability to share and understand each other would deepen beyond measure.

As it is, as long as they approach each other from their own frame of reference, in their own terms, in their own voices, they just will not be able to get through. They are not addressing each other's needs, they are not satisfying each other's wants, they are not even communicating with each other—*they are merely speaking to themselves.*

Each is addressing what he or she believes to be a copy of

his or her own temperament—not the other person's. Each is reacting solely to his or her own behavior pattern—not the other person's.

These are not two people talking *with each other.* These are two people each addressing a different—somehow off-key—version of themselves.

This erroneous belief that we are all speaking to nothing more than slightly different versions of ourselves can be seen all the time. It is most strikingly obvious when two people accuse each other of exactly the same thing—not realizing that, although each of them is saying the same thing, the meaning is completely different.

At one time or another all of us have been caught up in a variation of this sort of desperate, uncomprehending exchange with someone close to us—spouse, lover, friend, parent, or child:

> "You're so selfish—all you can think of is yourself. You never think of what I might want. I'm always trying to consider what you might what!"
>
> "How can *you* say that? Most of the time we spend doing things the way you want them done. My needs don't ever seem to count for anything. You never do anything the way *I* want. *You're* the self-centered one!"

Each of us is saying exactly the same thing and each of us believes it to be true. Each firmly believes we have been unselfishly meeting the other's needs. In a genuine attempt to satisfy the other person's wants, each has gone about it in the only way we each know how: by doing whatever it is that would have satisfied *our own* needs, and by saying what we should like to have heard said to *us.*

We don't realize that this is not the response the other person wants. We don't understand that this type of response *means nothing* to the other person: it does not satisfy his or her needs in the slightest. And his or her version of what we want is just as distorted.

Over and over, in every aspect of our lives, when we so genuinely believe we are being considerate, compassionate, caring, nurturing, supportive, and just plain loving to another, we are merely addressing ourselves. We are talking— not through malice but through ignorance—to no one but ourselves, and saying not what others want or need to hear, but what we need or would like to hear ourselves. So, not surprisingly, we remain alone and separate—sharing nothing, giving nothing, receiving nothing.

For all our prodigious advances in almost every field of human endeavor, we are still absymally ignorant about how human beings relate to each other. In the modern world, we spend so much time examining the Self we fail to realize that "me" is only half of "us." Each "me" remains an isolated, unsatisfied, and misunderstood social being, trying desperately to relate to other social beings who appear to be incomprehensible and consequently remain equally alone and lonely.

But human beings *are* understandable. We can understand them by simply understanding what their differences mean. These differences can be clearly recognized in their particular type of behavior, and this behavior, in turn, identifies the distinct way they think and feel.

There is a logical pattern to those differences in mental, physical, and verbal activity that is in fact recognizable, understandable, and, best of all, *predictable.* This means there is a way of understanding, responding to, and satisfying those needs of any person whose reciprocal understanding is important to us. A way of genuinely communicating with each other. A way of satisfying that basic human need we all have to share ourselves with someone who can understand us, whom we can understand in return.

It is a way that can be learned through the use of the step-by-step, simple, easily understood techniques set out in this book. These techniques include Look-Profiling Charts, which enable you to recognize and identify the personality types of the people who are important to you; Self-Identification Charts, to aid in the extremely difficult task of recognizing your own personality type, and seeing yourself as other see you; "Clash" Charts, to show exactly what it is about one personality that irritates and alienates another, and what can be done to turn that irritation and alienation into compassion, understanding, even love; and finally, a complete course in putting all these techniques and aids to work in your life and the lives of those you care for.

It is a complete course, if you like, in understanding the people around you who are most important to you, who and what they really are, and to understanding yourself for who and what you really are.

It will teach you to use and celebrate these differences in order to create, nurture, and sustain a firm, loving relationship, not in spite of these differences but because of them.

It can be summed up, in the first instance, in three simple words. Those words, the *3Rs* of all successful human relationships and communication, forming each of the three parts of this book, are: *Read, Respond, Reciprocate.*

They are the pivotal means by which people, so different and diverse, so apparently alien to each other, can at last actually speak not at each other but *with* each other.

# PART ONE

# "READ"

O N E

# The Four Personality Types: Feeler, Driver, Analyzer, Elitist

## "WHY CAN'T YOU BE MORE LIKE ME?": THE FUNDAMENTAL CAUSE OF OUR DIFFERENCES

"Why can't a woman be more like a man?" What Professor Higgins in *My Fair Lady* really meant by his exclamation of bewildered frustration at Eliza Doolittle was:

"Why can't you be more like me?"

"Why can't you *think* the way I do?"

"Why can't you *behave* more like me?"

We all splutter some variation of this theme when we have a "difference of opinion" with our lover, spouse, parents, or children. If only they would just think and act more like us, we would be able to understand them.

We tell ourselves we can't understand them, and they can't understand us, because of a difference of gender or age or background.

However, while it is so easy to blame these differences for our failure to understand each other and get along together, we often overlook the fact that there is a far more fundamental root cause for these differences. It is the difference in our personalities.

Our individual personalities are formed by definite groups of consistent traits or characteristics that *shape* those other—more superficial—differences of gender, age, or background. This particular group of traits—our personality *type*—runs across, beneath, and through all our superficial differences, and determines the way we think, feel, and behave, whether we are men or women, young or old—whatever our background. It dictates the way we face and deal with all the experiences of our lives, and shapes and colors our individuality. It is *who* we really are.

It is this personality type, with its innate, instinctive characteristics, which dictates our approach to life and relationships. It governs everything from our overt behavior, to the types of situation we are most comfortable in, to the sorts of people we are naturally attracted to, and everything we say, do, feel, and think through every aspect of our lives.

Everything a person does and says is explicable within the terms of his or her particular personality type—even down to the choice of clothing and color of tie.

### The Four Personality Types

There are only four basic personality types. Leaving aside people with personality disorders, we all instinctively act and react in accordance with the dictates of one—and only one—of these types.

These personality types are: The *Feeler,* the *Driver,* the *Analyzer,* the *Elitist.*

Each of these types has a recognizable, understandable, and predictable pattern of behavior—mental, verbal, and physical—which can be "read."

The first of the *3Rs* of *Read, Respond,* and *Reciprocate*—which are the fundamental techniques for creating and sustaining all successful relationships—is concerned with recognizing and identifying these patterns of behavior in any one person.

## "WHO ARE YOU, REALLY?": RECOGNIZING AND IDENTIFYING THE FOUR TYPES

In order to identify each of these types, we have to recognize the particular way each of them has of acting and reacting to the world and to the people around them.

The following brief outline sketches the distinctive traits of these four personality types that are the most clearly recognizable.

### The Feeler

The Feeler is the most commonly encountered of all four personality types and accounts for well over 50 percent of the population. The Feeler is an introvert, the sort of person you sense makes decisions about situations and relationships primarily by the way he or she *feels* about things. Feelers are generally quiet, laid back, warm, and often extremely considerate people. They listen carefully and patiently to others and seem to respond in a slower and more considered way than the other types. They rarely force their views on others; in fact, you may not even hear their personal opinion about something unless you ask what it is.

The character of Mary Richards, played by Mary Tyler Moore in the TV sitcom "The Mary Tyler Moore Show," is the quintessential Feeler. She *feels* for other people. In one episode Mary's boss, Lou (a Driver), is dejected because he has just seen his son-in-law out with another woman and he needs someone to talk to. He turns to Mary. Mary's reaction shows the depth of empathy a typical Feeler has for someone else's problems, and how the other person's pain even seems actually to be felt:

Lou: Oh . . . Mary . . .
Mary *(barely mouthing the words, consumed with inner pain):* I know . . .
Lou: Oh, Mary! Mary! Mary . . . !

Mary, with the expression on her face of a classical Greek mother discovering all her sons have been slaughtered, can merely repeat that she knows, she knows, she knows.

Choked with emotion, she positively oozes sympathy and understanding while barely saying a word. After a minute or so, Lou feels better about things and says, "Good. Thanks, Mary. That should do it."

He may have gotten over his distress, but she will feel it for him long after he has put it out of his mind.

The Feeler is unaggressive, dislikes conflict of any sort, and doubts his or her own ability to act successfully in a confrontational situation.

In another example, when Mary is moving into her new apartment, she comes face to face with Rhoda Morgenstern (another Driver), played by Valerie Harper, who wants the apartment herself. Rhoda hollers at Mary to get out as this is her apartment.

Mary suggests that Rhoda thinks she must be "some kind of pushover." Rhoda agrees in no uncertain terms, and Mary, halfheartedly mustering strength, replies:

Mary: Well, if you push I might just have to push back—hard.
Rhoda: Come on—you can't carry that off.
Mary *(shrugs sheepishly):* . . . I know. . . .

The integrity of the personality and the clarity of its portrayal in the fictional Mary Richards are the product of the writers' and Moore's brilliant observation of the behavior of real-life Feelers.

Dr. Martin Luther King, Jr., was a Feeler whose actions were shaped and forged in the only way his personality type allowed. Motivated by a passion to right the inequities of segregation, his plan for nonviolent struggle sprang from his Feeler's sensitivity to the pain caused by violence, his dread of confrontation, and his belief that human beings' strength lies in the power of feeling—the power of soul.

In a typical speech given in Birmingham, Alabama, in 1963, Dr. King said, "We will meet your physical force with soul force.

". . . We will wear you down by our capacity to suffer.

"In winning the victory, we will not only win our freedom, we will so appeal to your heart and your conscience, that we will win you in the process."

In July 1966, when he and the civil rights marchers faced attack from violently angry armed crowds in Chicago, Dr. King told his followers, "We are going to march with something much more powerful than that [Molotov cocktails, weapons, bricks, and bottles] . . . we are going to march with the force of our souls. . . ."

Like Dr. King, all Feelers believe that the most effective way of getting through to other people—of winning them over—is by appeal to their emotions, to their feelings.

---

**The Feeler:** Very private, quiet, and laid-back, emotionally sensitive, trusting, warm, sympathetic, and sincere, thoughtful and considerate, slower to react, nonconfrontational.

---

## The Driver

The Driver personality type—to whom the Feeler is often highly attracted—believes the exact opposite. The Driver deals in external information, giving credence only to what he or she can prove by observation empirically to be true. If the Driver wishes to appeal to another person, he or she does so not on the basis of feelings, but on the basis of facts.

The Driver is the extroverted type who you sense *has* to be in the driver's seat all the time, has to be in control of any situation or relationship, and who believes unshakably that without his/her hand on the wheel things are bound to go wrong. The Driver has but one aim in life, and that is to drive you to his/her way of thinking.

Drivers are vibrant, enthusiastic, lively, full of verve. They are quick-thinking and usually quick-talking people. They will give their views on any and every subject with perception and style—whether or not you want it.

Former New York City Mayor Ed Koch is a Driver type. His comment that in New York you "have to walk a little faster, talk a little faster and think a whole lot faster" epitomizes the way a Driver approaches life.

The Driver loves confrontation. It is a game, a duel of wits, and it has to be won. The character played by Candice Bergen in the TV sitcom "Murphy Brown" is pure Driver personality.

Faced with a rival anchorwoman at a reunion, Murphy immediately accuses her of plagiarizing the sign-off phrase "And so it goes," an accusation her rival, Linda, hotly denies. Linda blurts out that she didn't steal the phrase from Murphy, that she stole it from Lloyd Dobyns.

Murphy, in the Driver's spirit of verbal one-upmanship, throws back: "You're kidding! Gee, then I guess I should apologize for putting your name in the Personals Section of *Soldier of Fortune* magazine!"

However, Linda, who also happens to be a Driver type, with the Driver's need to come out on top in any battle of wits, replies without even taking time to draw breath, "No, we're even. I was the one who told Irving R. Levine you had the hots for him!"

The Driver's face is the most animated of all the personality types. Drivers are "actors" whose every emotion is graphically displayed, and whose body language is always used to reinforce what they're saying. One of the reasons for this was explained by a highly articulate Driver: "The audience makes me what I am—tells me when I'm a good person or a bad person. Either I'm dealing with an enraptured audience—in which case I'll do anything to please them—or I'm dealing with a heckler who has to be crushed, reduced to silence and disposed of as quickly as possible."

Being great manipulators who are constantly aware of how they are affecting others, Drivers may even alter both the tack of an argument and their demeanor in midsentence to achieve results if they feel the situation warrants it.

> **The Driver:** Quick-thinking and highly perceptive, enthusiastic, expressive and animated, controlling and manipulative, decisive, nonconforming, and confrontational.

### The Analyzer

The Driver characteristic of doing the manipulative quick-step contrasts strongly with the Analyzer trait of maintaining one and only one unwavering line of logical thought without any recourse to dramatic effect.

The Analyzer is an extroverted type, who you sense "analyzes" the pros and cons of situations and relationships, then makes decisions based on facts and logic.

He or she is the type of person you feel you can rely on in times of crisis always to remain level-headed and come up with a considered decision on what should be done. Analyzers rarely lose their cool, even when people all around them have lost theirs. While they may appear at times to enjoy lighthearted exchanges and frivolous situations, they never quite seem to participate wholeheartedly.

Barbara Walters, the renowned TV journalist, is an archetypical Analyzer. Her unflappability on air is well known. The Analyzer characteristics she brings to bear in her interviews are obvious: it is clear she has done her homework before every interview; each question is pointed and succinct; and she is not sidetracked by emotionality.

A writer on "The Today Show" who worked with her, in recalling their first meeting, is quoted as saying: "I noticed her eyes. I was impressed by the way she looked at you; her eyes were very enquiring. When she talked she looked straight into your eyes. When there was a pause you could see that the machinery in her head had been set in motion by what you told her. She was already organizing things, getting things done, moving forward."

The Analyzer, compared to other personality types, to quote Walters herself, is "much more concrete, much more interested in the here and now," and not at all concerned with the abstract.

An example, par excellence, of an Analyzer at work is the following diatribe, overheard being delivered by a professional gambler to a would-be blackjack player who was obviously a Feeler. This man refers to anyone who does not think and behave like an Analyzer as a "Sucker."

You're too emotional. You're a Sucker if you're too emotional. This is a game of logic! Logic must prevail in this game, not emotions.

If you make decisions based on emotions, you're a Sucker and the casinos love Suckers. They get rich off Suckers.

Use self-discipline. Control yourself. Don't play your hunches—be sensible!

Logic. Logic. Forget your emotions. Don't make decisions based on the "look" of the dealer, or the "feel" of the cards, or the fact that the lady next to you smiled at you—you'll lose.

Discipline yourself. Think logically. Work everything out logically, sequentially, calmly.

Like all professional gamblers, this man believes the only way to win at blackjack is to play the percentages; like all Analyzers, he believes it is the only way to win at Life.

> **The Analyzer:** Sensible and serious, focused and methodical, self-controlled and exacting, direct and assertive, very stable and unemotionally involved.

## The Elitist

The fourth personality type accounts for a small percentage of the population and is only rarely encountered. This is the Elitist, a person of great charm and style who may even be considered charismatic. While others may be drawn to this type of personality because of its charm and charisma, at base Elitists always appear to be somewhat aloof and "removed" from any situation or relationship they find themselves in.

Elitists rarely display extremes of behavior or emotion: they will not be heard raising their voices, cursing, disagreeing violently, laughing too loudly, behaving outrageously, or doing anything inappropriate.

They are loners, who seem to prefer to keep their real thoughts to themselves, often giving the unspoken impression that they are only truly comfortable with people they consider their intellectual peers.

A biographer of the Nobel Peace Prizewinner and roving diplomat Henry J. Kissinger describes his virtuoso style of diplomacy: "The same blend of humor and charm, toughness and candor, topped by no small amount of guile, characterizes his style with Congressmen and foreign leaders. He has the remarkable ability to convince two people with opposing viewpoints that he agrees with both of them—without in any way compromising his own position."

Elitists are aware of their own powerful egos and live with this aspect of themselves quite happily. The story is told that when someone at a Washington dinner party said, "Dr. Kissinger, I want to thank you for saving the world," Kissinger replied, "You're welcome."

> **The Elitist:** A loner. Charming, elegant and impressive, intellectually precise and insightful, aloof and condescending, dominant and dominating.

These sketches of the four basic personality types—the *Feeler,* the *Driver,* the *Analyzer,* and the *Elitist*—give only a general impression of the image each type projects. While the full personality picture will be revealed in due course, at this stage our purpose is simply to read and identify the personality type of a particular person.

Before moving on to identify, on a more intimate level, the personality types of the people you know well, here is a technique that is used to place the personality types of acquaintances or even strangers you are meeting for the first time.

## THE TEN-MINUTE LOOK-PROFILING TECHNIQUE: IDENTIFYING ANYONE'S PERSONALITY TYPE AT FIRST MEETING

This ten-minute technique is known as *Look Profiling.* It is a method of identifying someone's personality type swiftly, simply by observing him or her in any given situation. The more closely you observe—look, listen, and get a sense of— someone's actions and reactions, the more you realize just how much that person is actually revealing.

One word of warning: Look Profiling is not intended for self-identification. Do not try to recognize your own personality type this way.

LOOK PROFILING: Chart I *Identifying Personality Types*

|  | FEELER | DRIVER | ANALYZER | ELITIST |
|---|---|---|---|---|
| *Manner on entering room:* | Serious, somewhat reticent. Concerned about social comfort of others | Enthusiastically curious. Projection of image adopted for the occasion | Moderated and controlled mentally, physically, and verbally. Serious | Aloof, imperious. Superior person |
| *Initial conversational approach:* | Happiest with non-controversial small talk | Initiates conversation. Verbally and mentally quick. Very animated. Makes personal remarks about self | Makes careful small talk. Gives impression of wearing a "social" mask | Has strong sense of own prestige. Appears friendly but tries to establish "superior" position in relation to you |
| *Initial attitude toward you:* | Friendly, warm. Non-aggressive and non-confrontational | Overly friendly. Naturally gregarious person | Pleasant but rather distant and self-contained | Considerate and pleasant but aloof. Very observant. Somewhat detached from whole setting |
| *Personality characteristics that emerge in first few minutes:* | Private person. Would be happiest in small groups. Not pushy—will take back seat in conversation. Not aggressive in expressing personal point of view | Quick-talking, quick-thinking. Very perceptive. Nonconformist. Likes to be in control of the situation | Has an intellectual rather than an emotional response to life. Not particularly at ease in lighthearted or frivolous situations. Very self-confident | Has an "aura" of being someone special, often charismatic. Will stand out in crowd by elegance, bearing, taste, and manners |

The preceding Look-Profiling Chart for identifying strangers focuses on the impression transmitted by each type as he or she comes into a room or enters into conversation with you in a normal, unstressful social setting. Reading these transmitted signals will enable you to identify the type with 85 to 90 percent accuracy.

To use the Look-Profiling Chart, first read each column separately from top to bottom to get an overall picture of each personality type.

Next, read *across* the columns to compare and contrast the distinctive way each personality type behaves and the very different impression you get of each.

T W O

# How to Read
# the Personality Types
# of the People You Care For

## "WHY DON'T I BELIEVE YOU REALLY CARE FOR ME?": DIFFERENT TYPES OF LOVING

Often we can't understand why the people we care for deeply aren't loving us the way we want to be loved. At times, because they are not behaving in what we consider to be a loving way, we even tell ourselves they don't really love us.

However, in recognizing how different their personality types are from ours, we realize that their view of what constitutes love, and what constitutes their loving us, may not be the same as what we believe constitutes love and how we want to be loved.

Yet their view and behavior are as much an integral part of their whole personality as ours is of our own personality.

Identifying the "whole" personality type of the people we care for is the most important and vital step of the first of the *3Rs: Read.*

An example of the fact that we all love differently according to our individual personality types, and of how that difference can make a person feel painfully alone and isolated within a relationship, is illustrated by the following true story.

Helen and her husband, Bob, both in their mid-forties, own and run a profitable hardware store in a small midwestern town. Helen is a Feeler and Bob is a Driver. They have been married for twenty-five years and have one child, a daughter, Patty.

Helen's niggling sense of alienation and loneliness within her own family always stemmed from the fact that Patty seemed to have a much closer and more understanding relationship with her father than she ever had with Helen.

She relates a typical example of this alienation that happened when Patty was about three years old. Bursting with exciting news, the child rushed into the store office and began telling it to her father, who was in the middle of a telephone conversation with a customer.

Bob, putting his hand over the mouthpiece of the phone, shouted at her: "Quiet—not now! Go away!"

Patty turned and skipped out of the office, not the least put out by being dismissed so summarily.

Helen, who was also present at the time, watched the child go, astonished at her reaction. She herself, in her Feeler way, even as an adult, would have been cut to the quick by such treatment. Had her own father shouted at her that way as a three-year-old child, she would have dissolved into tears on the spot.

Rushing out of the office after Patty, Helen caught up with her to comfort her and explain that her father was just busy, he wasn't really angry at her.

But Patty didn't need comforting. She wasn't upset at all.

Later, when Helen asked Bob not to shout at the child like that, he looked at *her* in surprise and said, "Don't be silly. She knows I didn't mean anything by it." And obviously, Patty did know that.

Incidents like this of Bob and Patty "obviously knowing" what each other meant—and Helen consistently *not* knowing or misinterpreting what they. meant—were repeated so often as Patty grew up that Helen began to feel she was "the odd man out," on a completely different wavelength from her husband and daughter.

Over and over, in incident after incident, she felt more and more like an outsider in her own family.

She sensed this particularly if she happened to join in with her husband and daughter when they were deep in discussion, or playing a game, or simply kidding around. She felt she was intruding, and realized they both changed their approach to accommodate her. When she joined them, their conversation slowed down, they toned down their rapid-fire retorts, and actually stopped cutting off the ends of each other's sentences the way they did when she wasn't involved. Even the way they played board games together became less aggressive and fiercely competitive when she joined in.

Helen believed she was "cramping their style" when she was with them, and assumed they both regarded her as somehow "superfluous," so eventually she was reluctant to join in at all.

Because she obviously did not think the way they both did, Helen sometimes felt very alone and shut out. She noticed that Patty was always more comfortable dealing with situations the way Bob advised rather than any way she might suggest. She began to stop trusting her own judgment about what would and would not please them, and took to asking each of them what they thought the other's reaction would be to everything from presents to what to do on vacation.

She couldn't help wondering if Patty really loved her father more than she loved her mother. And she couldn't, for the life of her, think what to do about it.

Helen also felt that being unable to establish the same

closeness that Bob had, she had somehow failed to "be there" for her daughter. She believed she had not been a good mother, and felt deeply guilty about it.

She assumed their rapport was something to do with "blood line or heredity," and that really she had to accept the fact that, however hard she might try, she could never be as close to her daughter as Bob was. Even though her family life was very happy overall, Helen frequently got a feeling of unease that something was "wrong" or "incomplete" within the family circle. Being a Feeler, she assumed it was her fault.

But Helen, the Feeler, kept all her nagging feelings of confusion, alienation, and guilt deeply hidden. She did not even discuss them with Bob, as she knew he would tell her they were unfounded and ridiculous. She certainly did not mention them to her daughter, as she didn't want Patty to feel she had failed her mother in any way. She just lived with them bottled up inside her and believed that was the way things would always be, until she was introduced to the *3Rs*.

Then, in the *Read* stage of the *3Rs,* Helen identified both Bob and Patty as Driver personality types. She suddenly saw how and why they both reacted to everything the same way as the other. She saw how they actually did *think* the same way.

She, as a Feeler, simply did not think the same way, and therefore she didn't act or react the way they did. She *couldn't.* Any more than they could think the way she did.

There was no "conspiracy" to shut her out—neither of them could help being the way they were any more than she could help being the way she was. Bob and Patty *were* in fact "on the same wavelength," not out of perversity or intention or even thoughtlessness—they simply shared the same personality type.

Helen said it was like suddenly seeing the light. Her sense of relief at knowing that there was nothing "wrong" with her was unbelievably liberating. Patty had never followed her suggestions on how to deal with things because she was unable to think and feel about things the way Helen did—not because she had thought her mother was "less intelligent, or less astute, or less sensitive" than her father. Her incredible rapport with Bob had been simply because they both thought the same way.

Thinking about it in light of the characteristics of the Driver type, Helen began to see that her daughter loved her in the only way her personality type allowed, which—while different from the way Helen expected and wanted to be loved—was just as deep and just as true a way of loving.

She began to wonder what else she had simply assumed—incorrectly—about her daughter, her husband, and even herself.

## NO-HOLDS-BARRED ARGUMENTS: THE EMERGENCE OF THE CORE PERSONALITY TYPE

Helen was aware that her husband and daughter altered or toned down their "natural" behavior when she joined them. They did it to make her feel more comfortable and include her within the family circle.

As social beings, we all modify our behavior to accommodate the people we care for, simply because we like being with them and want to be accepted by them. We become more thoughtful and considerate of their comfort and feelings, and we instinctively act and react in a way we know they find appealing and understandable.

When we modify our behavior to suit them, we cloak or mask our true personality to some extent. While our real personality still shines through, it becomes toned down and less explicit.

There is, however, one particular time when our personality type is not toned down or masked or camouflaged in any way. That is when we are under attack, and particularly under very personal verbal attack.

The classic example of this is a no-holds-barred argument or family dispute.

Stress hits us and we fight back. We react instinctively to protect ourselves and defeat our attacker—and we use whatever method works best for us. We do what comes naturally.

What comes naturally to the surface then is our "core" personality. All the pure characteristics of our type emerge in sharp relief and at full strength. Our rawest behavior is on display: it is unavoidably obvious and very easy to read.

## LOOK PROFILING THE PERSONALITY TYPES OF THE PEOPLE YOU LOVE

The following Look-Profiling Chart for rapidly identifying the personality types of the people you care for is based on recognizing the distinctive characteristics they display when they feel they are under attack in the middle of an intense argument.

This identification technique is on a far more intimate, indepth level than the last one for observing the "controlled" social behavior of people you are meeting for the first time.

It draws on your own, very private knowledge of how the person you are going to identify reacts when he or she is arguing with *you*.

Again, this is not a self-identification technique. Do not try to identify your own personality type from this chart. The next chapter shows you how to identify your own type.

To use the chart, first read each column separately, top to bottom, to get the overall picture of each personality type.

Next, read *across* the columns to compare and contrast the distinctive way each personality type behaves when in conflict with another person.

LOOK PROFILING: Chart II *Identifying Personality Types in Conflict*

|  | FEELER | DRIVER | ANALYZER | ELITIST |
|---|---|---|---|---|
| *Demeanor or image presented:* | Emotionally involved. Defensive of situation. Slower reactions than other types. Hates confrontation of any sort. Doubts own courage | Enthusiastically and dramatically involved. Ready for the attack. Argument is a game—to be won. Rapid reactions. Needs to control situation and you | Analytical, calculating. Emotionally uninvolved. Detached from fault or guilt—the problem is yours, not his/hers. Underlying aggression | Superior, "this is beneath me" attitude. Someone, something else to blame for problem—definitely not him/her. Dominating attitude |
| *Offensive/Defensive method of attack:* | Primary defensive. Reacts rather than instigates. At start of stress pulls into Denial. Overly serious. Listens intently, tries to be patient. Needs to know your position and reasoning before hitting back. May agree just to defuse argument. | Eagerly offensive. Wants complete and total directional control of argument. Picks up what you are aiming at quickly. Will focus on that part of your argument which shows weakness. Uses anger as power over you. | Calculatingly offensive. Deadly serious. Dogmatic. Own reasoning and logic crystal clear; if you can't see it as obviously, you are at fault. Shows no remorse unless problem is one he/she has obviously caused. | Offensive when attacked. Challenges when threatened—otherwise removed from problem. Knows exactly what you're talking about, but says does not understand or relate to your point. Has to dominate you and situation. |

*continued on following pages*

LOOK PROFILING: **Chart II** *Identifying Personality Types in Conflict (cont.)*

|  | FEELER | DRIVER | ANALYZER | ELITIST |
|---|---|---|---|---|
| *Offensive/Defensive method of attack (cont.):* | Will not attack head-on, usually attacks peripherally. Stores up comments for counterattack, rather than inter-jecting constantly. Narrows down what you say to a few comments | Swings between ex-treme positions, rarely takes moder-ate position. Is impatient when you talk and inter-jects comments. Talks too much. Nitpicks your rea-soning | Responds quickly to a slight—real or imagined. Subconsciously checks your com-ments—if does not consider them or-derly and precise, will tell you so. Wants to know why he/she is being asked or told to do some-thing or answer a question | Always on guard against losing self-control. Talks too much about his/her own problems |
| *Responses: (i) Emotional:* | Totally emotionally involved. Cannot handle emo-tional pain or any de-gree of anger aimed at him/her. If considers stress to be unfair will fall to pieces. Dislikes theatrics, loudness, or anger—will shut down and withdraw into self | Excitable. Overly dramatic and theatrical verbally. Swings through moods rapidly. Pulls into anger very quickly | Views emotion as weakness to be ex-ploited. Puzzled and put out by emotionality | Appears emotionally restless |

3 6

| | | | | |
|---|---|---|---|---|
| *(ii) Intellectual:* | Dominating mood is Bargaining. Emotions distort ability to think logically. If not approached in same mood or channel, what you say will not compute intellectually. Craves to be validated, credited for who he/she is | Dominating mood is Anger. Rapid intellectual activity. Makes up mind quickly on what has happened to cause the problem. Always "right" in stress situations. His/her way is the *only* correct way; you are stupid if you do not agree. Will lie verbally to prove a point. Uses personal reasoning (unrelated to objective logic) to drive you to his/her way of thinking | Dominating mood is Denial. Pure intellectual response to stress. Controls own anger through logic. Feels he/she is in the "eye of the hurricane" while others rage all around | Dominating mood is Depression. Feels intellectually superior. Thinks about what may occur in relationship, or what will occur as a result of argument |
| *(iii) Physical:* | Primary direction of eye movement: to the *left.* Body language very pronounced, indicative of varying emotional state | Primary direction of eye movement: to the *right.* Body language animated, dramatic, and theatrical, used to overemphasize points and to manipulate you | Primary direction of eye movement: to the *right.* Body language very controlled. Latent aggression | Primary direction of eye movement: to the *right.* Never does anything "gross" in conflict. May appear to be momentarily hypnotized—has mentally shut down |

Then, using this knowledge, identify the types of the particular individuals you have in mind.

If there is still any doubt in your mind about which personality type the person you want to identify is, reread the chart carefully.

A person cannot be a combination of types. Each individual is one type and one only.

Remember, this chart works if you are identifying someone you care for *and* if you have been involved in a serious argument with that someone. If you are having difficulty recognizing a particular person, you may not care for him or her, or you may not have been involved in the sort of "raw" conflict that is required to bring out his or her pure personality traits.

If this is the case, rely on the first Look-Profiling Chart (p. 27) to identify their type, and read on with that type in mind to understand exactly *who* the individual really is, even though that person may not have fully revealed him- or herself to you yet.

## "While in the Guise of . . ."

In public, people have to wear the style of clothing dictated by the (image) demands of their jobs or peer groups.

In private, however, they are free to wear, not the uniform dictated by their occupations, superiors, or "place in society," but whatever they feel most comfortable and at home in.

They wear the clothes that reflect their own personalities.

**Feelers** favor warm, neutral, earthy, or subdued tones, in styles that are not overly revealing of their presence, their opinions, or their bodies. They like to blend in.

**Drivers** prefer bright or positive colors, in sometimes unconventional, eye-catching styles that assert their individuality. Women Drivers, especially, like to stand out in a crowd.

**Analyzers** like more conventional, functional, no-nonsense clothing. Their choice of what they wear always makes sense for the occasion—whether relaxing, gardening, playing with the children, or doing an oil change on the car. Above all, they are "logical" in their choice of what to wear.

**Elitists** invariably demonstrate style, elegance, and perfect taste in even their most casual attire. Their choice may at times be somewhat idiosyncratic, but it is always indisputably "appropriate."

In any relationship, embryonic or long term, if you're not sure you're seeing the real person, noting how they dress when they are casually "being themselves" offers a reliable way of identifying their personality type and seeing who they *really* are.

# THREE

# How to Read Your Own Personality Type

## "I KNOW EXACTLY WHO I AM—OR DO I?": THE PROBLEMS OF SEEING OURSELVES CLEARLY

Learning to recognize and accept your own personality type—the next step—can be rather more demanding than identifying another person's type.

All of us have lived intimately with ourselves all our lives, so nobody could ever know us better than we know ourselves.

Whatever our age, we've all been exposed to the "me" generation, to books on self-awareness, to magazine articles exhorting us to "get in touch with our feelings," and to a seemingly endless barrage of print and media programs entreating us in one way or another to "know ourselves."

We've analyzed our own motives, studied our own behavior, and been pushed mercilessly to see ourselves as we really are—warts and all.

So we know exactly what makes us tick. We know exactly who we really are.

Or do we?

If we really do know ourselves so well, why can't we identify our own personality type clearly in either of the Look-Profiling Charts we've just looked at? We can identify the people close to us quickly enough; but when it comes to recognizing our own type, we find that we don't fit neatly into any one category—rather, we see something of ourselves in all four of the types.

From the first Look-Profiling Chart (p. 27), we may find ourselves to be "warm and friendly," like the Feeler type; "very perceptive," like the Driver type; "moderated and controlled mentally," like the Analyzer type; and, lifted directly from the Elitist type, "someone special." From the second chart (pp. 35–37), we may think that, when arguing with someone, we "listen patiently" (Feeler type); "pick up the point quickly" (Driver type); "control our anger" (Analyzer type); and again lifted directly from that rarest of all types, the Elitist, "never do anything gross."

We sound wonderful. We are in fact the nicest person we have ever met in our lives, with nothing but the best features of every other type on earth.

And that's the problem.


## "But I Did It Because . . .": How We All Justify Our Own Behavior

We don't see ourselves as having any major faults because, as Mark Twain commented, "A man cannot be comfortable without his own approval." In order to make living with ourselves bearable, we have to be comfortable with who we are and approve of ourselves—and we do so, almost without reservation.

The few faults we do admit to having, we see in a very different light from the way other people view them. Where they may be hard and critical of us, we are never hard or critical of ourselves. On the contrary, we find it easy to justify our actions to ourselves, and have become masters at rationalizing, projecting, and minimizing our character flaws. After all, we have been practicing it since childhood.

We learn early on how to rationalize our behavior by devising plausible explanations to excuse it. A child being scolded for hurting his little sister may blurt out: "But I had to trip her up. If I hadn't been so quick-thinking, she could have chased the ball into the street and gotten hit by a giant tractor-trailer—and then I wouldn't even *have* a little sister!"

He knows this explanation isn't true. She was just annoying him and he wanted her to stop—so he tripped her up. But, knowing this was wrong, he has to justify his behavior somehow, and once he's concocted the right rationalization for wantonly assaulting his sister, it sounds so good he'll probably believe it himself and even become indignant when his parents don't.

The child also discovers the benefits to himself of minimizing his behavior by making it appear as unimportant as possible: "But she only bumped her head on the sidewalk anyway. It's not as if she's got any broken bones or blood pouring out!"

His self-justification increases further if he can project the blame onto someone else: "But really it was *her* fault anyway—if she hadn't been teasing me, she wouldn't have gotten me so mad at her in the first place." He may even kick at the ball his sister was playing with, saying: "This dumb ball is too big for her to handle anyway!"

By the time we have reached adulthood, we all have this technique of self-justification down to a fine art. We can forgive ourselves almost anything.

As adults, we have no difficulty forgiving ourselves in those relationships with our spouses or lovers where we are most desperate not to appear at fault. We find we can rationalize away all our misdeeds. We say, "I'm not apologizing—my actions were perfectly justified in the circumstances. Look at it this way. . . ."

We can even minimize our offenses: "This is the first time since our wedding that I've been unfaithful. It's not as if I play around all the time like most people we know," while glibly projecting the blame elsewhere: "And it's really your fault, anyway—you were flirting with everyone at the party. None of this would have happened it you'd had more self-control." Or even: "Those damn parties—there's always too much liquor!"

We have all been justifying ourselves with such skill for so long that by adulthood we have actually begun to believe our own self-serving view of ourselves. We have convinced ourselves that our thoughts and feelings are so high-minded, right, and snow white blameless that anyone who doesn't see things the way we do must be being either dimwitted, demented, or just purposely perverse.

## PERSONALITY IS IN THE EYE OF THE BEHOLDER: WHY WE CAN'T JUST GUESS OUR OWN TYPE

Unfortunately for us, however, other people are not being dimwitted, demented, or perverse.

Since they are not as privy to our particular thoughts and feelings as we are, they don't see us the way we see ourselves at all. They don't see our behavior in our terms of reference—they see it in their own. And they cannot be as forgiving of us as we are of ourselves.

Each of the personality types sees his or her own characteristic way of thinking and acting in self-justifying terms, and has no trouble rationalizing, projecting, and minimizing those traits that others may consider irritating flaws of character.

For instance, if we are *Feelers*, we have no difficulty in seeing ourselves as being conciliatory, thoughtful, and kind.

Other personality types—considering our behavior and attitudes in *their* terms—might see us as being merely indecisive, slow, and saccharine.

If we are *Drivers,* we readily justify our direct and outspoken behavior to ourselves because we see ourselves as being more perceptive, decisive, and forceful than other people. Others, however, viewing our behavior from their own perspective, see us merely as opinionated, controlling, and overbearing.

If we are *Analyzers,* we think of ourselves as being logical, orderly, and consistent, whereas other types may think of us less forgivingly as merely cold, heartless, and calculating.

If we are *Elitists,* we believe we are charming, controlled, and deserving of respect, but others may believe us to be merely aloof, arrogant, and self-satisfied.

So who is right? "We" or "They"?

Unfortunately, it is "They."

Personality is not in the eye of the holder, it is in the eye of the beholder. The ability to see ourselves through the eyes of that beholder is the only way we are ever going to be able to communicate with that less forgiving person we face whose understanding means so much to us.

## "I THOUGHT YOU LIKED THE WAY I AM": THE WAY OTHERS REALLY SEE US

While we are all aware of some of the unflattering opinions others hold of us, all of us fail to realize the *full* extent of others' attitudes from those few unpleasant signals we do pick up.

For example, in "The Mary Tyler Moore Show," when Mary Richards (a Feeler) confronts Rhoda Morgenstern (a Driver) over the disputed apartment, she is aware that Rhoda sees her as a "pushover." But is she aware that Rhoda also sees her as being so "soft" that she can either walk all over Mary at will or be forced to feel guilty at her own easy abuse of dominance over Mary and take pity on her?

Mary sees herself as being patient, thoughtful, and considerate. Rhoda sees her as being none of these things. She only sees someone who is all too easy to manipulate.

Similarly, Rhoda thinks of herself as assertive, outgoing, and persuasive. Mary, on the other hand, sees her only as pushy and controlling: a bully.

Although this sitcom scene is lighthearted and the viewer sees the funny side of the personality clash, all amusement vanishes when the scene is transferred to real life with a similar personality clash between husband and wife over disputes such as who does what, how the vacations should be spent, how the kids are to be raised, and even how to express that basic, desperate need they have for each other.

These clashes between very different personalities can only be kept lighthearted and within manageable bounds when each type understands how he or she appears to another type.

When we can see ourselves the way others see us, we can identify our own personality type with as much ease as we identified the personality types of those closest to us.

## "IS THAT WHAT YOU REALLY THINK OF ME?": HOW TO SEE OURSELVES THROUGH OTHERS' EYES

To see ourselves from this perspective, we have to step outside ourselves and see ourselves as others see us—warts and all; and even then the warts they see may not be the same ones we think we have. We have to be unflinchingly honest and look at ourselves with clearsighted objectivity. And while we may not like some of the things that we discover about ourselves and the way others see us, this is nevertheless the only way we are going to understand why people react to our personality the way they do.

In order to see ourselves clearly as others see us, we must *contrast* what we think and feel about our behavior with the reactions to that behavior we get from other people.

It is easiest to recognize the way we think and feel under stress—especially when we argue with someone who is close and important to us—as this is when the "core" of our personality is being drawn on and our uncontrolled "true" mental and emotional patterns are on display.

Although all of us, whatever our personality type, go through some sort of denial, anger, and depression when we are in intense conflict with someone we love, each type displays these emotions differently.

As the person we are arguing with is also under stress, this is also the time when we will hear *their* uncontrolled, "true" reactions to the way we behave when we display or control these emotions.

The following four Self-Identification Charts illustrate both the inner workings of each of the personality types and the outer reflections of them as seen through others' eyes. They highlight how we see ourselves while characterizing how others see us.

First, read the column which details how *you believe* you react when you think and feel you are under attack.

If you agree that this is how you react in stress, then read the next column, which details how others see your behavior—from their perspective. While they may be too polite actually to make some of these comments to your face, they will definitely be thinking them!

## How to Know If You Are a Feeler

Those of us who are *Feelers* usually consider other people's needs before our own. We are happiest when everybody gets what they want and there is no friction. When asked what we want to do, we frequently say something like: "Whatever you want is fine with me . . ."

Believing we are being considerate and generous-spirited, we are deeply hurt when we hear unjustified comments like: "Don't you ever have an opinion of your own?" "Why do you let everybody walk all over you?" "Why can't you ever say what you think directly?" or even, "What a wimp!"

If you are prone to using expressions like "Whatever you want is fine with me . . . ," but are constantly being accused of being too ready to agree, and feel you are being concilia-tory and considerate when all around berate you instead for being inert and insipid, then you are probably the Feeler per-sonality type, illustrated in the chart on pages 48–50.

## HOW TO KNOW IF YOU ARE A DRIVER

Those of us who are *Driver* types, on the other hand, who always have an instinctive urge to express ourselves openly and let others know just what it is we think about things, routinely exasperate other people who think our behavior is immoderate or over-the-top compared to their own. There are times when, to them, everything we do or say seems overdramatic to the point of sensationalism.

The Murphy Brown character (a Driver) is having a partic-ularly trying day when everything in life is irritating her—and she is saying so. To cap it off, she hears that the powers-that-be are concerned about her appearance on camera: overweight and pregnant.

Unable to contain her indignation, Murphy rails at her pro-ducer, Miles, that she cannot believe that after fifteen years with the network she would be subjected to something as hu-miliating, as ridiculous, as *degrading*, as an Appearance Clause.

Miles, who has had just about all he can take of her way of letting her feelings be known, finally says: "Murphy, could

| WHEN: | YOU BELIEVE: | BUT OTHERS SAY OR THINK: |
|---|---|---|
| *Conflict Is Brewing* | You have a highly developed sensitivity to others' emotional unease. | "Stop being the little friend of all the world." |
| | You are always alert to signs of tension or strain between people. | "You don't have to shoulder everyone else's problems." |
| | You can sense where a problem is, where fault lies, where threat is coming from, where pain and hurt are involved. | "What are you so concerned about—it's not your problem." |
| | You are particularly aware of the fairness/unfairness of any accusations that are being thrown out. | "Relax, don't worry so much." |
| | You try to soothe ruffled feathers; try to stop conflict before it escalates by being conciliatory. | "Stop worrying about what I think—tell me what you think yourself!" |
| *Conflict Begins* | You should not react immediately—unless an attack is grossly unfair. | "Say something! Don't you have an opinion?" |
| | You should hear and understand other's point of view before drawing a conclusion. | "Stop being such a wimp—why don't you fight back?" |
| | You must listen to and watch other carefully, with patience and an open mind, and draw conclusions on how deeply he/she may be affected by the conflict. | "Stop saying what you think I want to hear—tell me what *you* think!" |
| | | "You're too *nice!*" |
| | You consider it more important to know how other feels emotionally about the situation rather than what he/she may think of the facts of the conflict. | "Don't you feel strongly about anything? Why aren't you reacting to what I'm saying?!" |
| | | "You're too easily dominated—what a pushover!" |
| | You must not allow your own feelings to show as this may cause a strong reaction. You try to project warmth, kindness, and understanding. | "Why do you believe everything anyone tells you? Do you have to be so gullible?" |

You should give the other the benefit of the doubt until you understand the problem.
You should wait until you have all the information before deciding on your own stance, so you will listen to tedious, boring, complicated comments from the other without interjecting.
You wait until you feel you do understand all relevant information, then decide on your own position and plan how to attack the problem so as to solve it with least hurt.

You are forced to counterattack immediately with a strong emotional response if the attack on you is grossly unfair.

"Stop reacting so emotionally!"

*Conflict Is in Full Swing*

That other is the aggressor and you have to defend yourself against attack.
That, having carefully decided on your position, you will only be swayed by very convincing factual or emotional evidence.
You need to respond more to the degree of pain shown by the other than to any logical argument he/she may present. You are more interested in how the other feels about the conflict than in the facts of the conflict.
You should never approach a problem head-on as you feel this may cause too dramatic a reaction. You think an oblique approach would be more productive.

"I'm not attacking you personally, I'm disagreeing with what you say!"
"You're so stubborn—once you've decided how you feel nothing shifts you!"
"Will you stop asking me how I *feel* about it— that's not what's at issue here!"
"How much more of this emotional touchie-feelie garbage do I have to put up with?!"
"Stop concentrating on minor irrelevancies— get to the point!"
"For heaven's sake, stop being nice when I'm chewing you out!"
"I can never tell what you're thinking! *Say* something, will you!"

*continued on following page*

4 9

| WHEN: | YOU BELIEVE: | BUT OTHERS SAY OR THINK: |
|---|---|---|
| *Conflict Is in Full Swing (cont.)* | You should concede small points to try to win other people over, to show you understand their pain, to be fair, and to stop escalation. You are being hemmed in and cornered: if being overdominated, if not being given a fair chance to explain your position in your own way, and if not being given the same sympathetic, open-minded hearing you have given the other. | "Stop being so emotional!" "Stop being so irrational!" "Get a grip on yourself!" |
| | That at this point, because of the unfairness of the situation, your emotional response is justified in overtaking any rational response you might have had. | |
| | That, because of the other's unfairness all empathy has been destroyed, and you have difficulty comprehending other's remarks and interacting with other's comments in any but an emotional way. | |

| | AND AS A FEELER, AS A RESULT, YOU: | AND THEN YOU HEAR: |
|---|---|---|
| | Feel victimized. Shut down and close other out so as not to lose control, or Lose control and become hysterical, or Turn in on yourself with depression. | "You're not even listening to me anymore, are you?" "You've shut me out, haven't you?" "Don't fall to pieces!" "Stop being hysterical!" "You're just feeling sorry for yourself!" |

you maybe limit your anger to maybe one topic per day? The anchor desk, the Appearance Clause, people at the cash machines who forget their secret codes—pick one!"

If Murphy's attitude strikes a sympathetic chord with you and her behavior seems perfectly understandable, you are probably all too familiar with accusations that you are melodramatic, too quick to anger, and never shut up long enough to let other people have a say. Then you are definitely a Driver personality type.

The following Self-Identification Chart for the Driver (pp. 52–54) highlights the way those of us who are Drivers think when in stress, at the same time illustrating the reactions of other people—who are not privy to our motivations—to our personality.

## How to Know If You Are an Analyzer

Those of us who have *Analyzer* personality types have all been subjected to a variation of the charge leveled at Barbara Walters: that she is "steellike, hard, even insensitive."

We consider this attitude extremely unfair. To our minds, our feelings and emotional responses are our own business and no one else's. We can deal with them very well in private without displaying them to the world at large, and we secretly think that people who make a big show of their feelings are revealing a total lack of self-control and are rather weak individuals.

We know that allowing our emotions to get the better of us interferes with our ability to think clearly and get on with the job of solving any problem that arouses painful feelings in us.

Barbara Walters, in an interview with Merv Griffin, explained the Analyzer's point of view in these terms: "When this kind of criticism hit in the beginning I cried, silently. And I think that's what saved me. I didn't cry on the air and I didn't whine. Now I don't bleed as much as I did. . . . And I

**Self-Identification Chart**
*YOU ARE A DRIVER IF*

| WHEN: | YOU BELIEVE: | BUT OTHERS SAY OR THINK: |
|---|---|---|
| *Conflict Is Brewing* | You have a highly developed awareness of reactions being wrong and want to step in and sort things out quickly.<br><br>You can disperse ill-feeling rapidly with logic, clever use of words, and even humor.<br><br>You can maneuver the other into Acceptance with quick skill, perception, and awareness of how to stop hurt or mounting annoyance | "You never know when to leave well enough alone—this has nothing to do with you!"<br><br>"Stop being so controlling!"<br><br>"Will you stop trying to tell me what I should think!"<br><br>"You always have too much to say for yourself!" |
| *Conflict Begins* | You can see the direction conflict is taking more clearly and quickly than the other.<br><br>You are immediately aware of possible solutions.<br><br>You know the direction argument should go and how to resolve it.<br><br>You can explain positions clearly and succinctly so both of you can work through this quickly and get it sorted out.<br><br>Other has tendency to miss the point and wander off in the wrong direction so you try repeatedly to bring him/her back on track.<br><br>That other never appears to be listening to you or hearing what you are saying.<br><br>You have to keep changing tack until you get the desired response | "What makes you think you have the only right answer to everything!"<br><br>"Stop trying to manipulate me—just because I don't agree with you it doesn't mean I'm wrong!"<br><br>"Stop rushing me—give me time to think!"<br><br>"I heard you the first time—you don't have to keep repeating things over and over!"<br><br>"Will you stop interrupting—let me finish!"<br><br>"Just stick to the point and stop jumping all over the place!" |

| Conflict Is in Full Swing | |
|---|---|
| That once other is able to understand your reasoning and see the obvious solution he/she will agree with you.<br><br>You should use any ploy to get it through to him/her: verbal, emotional, logical—whichever works best.<br><br>You are justified in using white lies to make your point clearer or get the other back on track when necessary.<br><br>You should be dramatic in delivery as this will make your point more emotionally and rationally powerful.<br><br>That other's inability to follow what you're getting at, to keep up with you, to meet your points as quickly and succinctly as you would want, forces you to lose patience.<br><br>You must strenuously resist other's attempts to take control of the direction of the argument or to manipulate you.<br><br>That when the other concentrates on irrelevant details you have to keep trying to bring him/her back on track, even though you find this increasingly exasperating. | "You're overwhelming me—give me time to think!"<br>"Why can't you ever just say you're sorry?"<br>"You don't have to lie to prove your point!"<br>"Calm down. You don't have to be so melodramatic about everything!"<br>"Why do you go from one extreme to the other? There is a middle way."<br>"Stop telling me to 'Hurry up' and 'Get on with it!'"<br>"Why does *everything* make you so angry?!"<br>"What I'm saying could be right, you know! What makes you think you always have the only right answers?"<br>"You haven't heard a thing I've said! *Listen* to me!"<br>"You're the most overbearing, controlling person I've ever come across!"<br>"This isn't some sort of game—it's serious!"<br>"Why do you always have to make fun of what I say?" |

*continued on following page*

SELF-IDENTIFICATION/DRIVER *(cont.)*

| WHEN: | YOU BELIEVE: | BUT OTHERS SAY OR THINK: |
|---|---|---|
| *Conflict Is in Full Swing (cont.)* | That when the other tries to turn the dispute into a personal attack on you, you have a right to counterattack with greater force than has been directed at you.<br><br>That if the pace is too slow, the information too uninteresting, or the opponent too easy to beat, it is not worth your while continuing with the argument | "What makes you think you have some sort of right to talk more than I do and always have the last word?"<br><br>"Are you *bored* with this?" |

| | AND AS A DRIVER, AS A RESULT, YOU: | AND THEN YOU HEAR: |
|---|---|---|
| | Hit back too hard and attack any weakness in the other where it hurts most.<br>Cannot help saying things you regret almost immediately.<br>Become indignant that the other cannot understand what you are getting at and lose patience completely.<br>Either vent your anger with vehemence, or become depressed at the outcome of the conflict and your own inability to handle it correctly | "Why do you end up saying the cruelest, most hurtful thing you can think of?!"<br>"You know that's not true—why do you have to say things like that?!"<br>"Calm down! Your anger is *too* extreme—you're crazy!"<br>"Stop feeling sorry for yourself!"<br>"You're just sulking because you lost the argument!" |

think the only thing you can do in my position is continue to do your work and do it as well as you can."

However, people who are not aware of the internal pain of Analyzers (Analyzers are masters at not showing such pain in their behavior) misinterpret this behavior as being merely cold, unfeeling, impersonal, and hard.

The following Self-Identification Chart for the Analyzer describes the way Analyzers think when in an argument with someone close to them, together with the types of accusations that are directed at their behavior by those who are not aware of how they are thinking.

If you typically think this way in similar situations and have been the brunt of the types of comments noted in the chart on pages 56–57, then you are an Analyzer.

## HOW TO KNOW IF YOU ARE AN ELITIST

Those of us who are *Elitists* are aware that others cannot really make us out, that we appear enigmatic to most people. But that impression suits us just fine. We prefer to keep people at arm's length anyway and have very few intimate relationships.

Henry Kissinger (an Elitist) has been called a "charming hieroglyphic." When asked by the Italian journalist Oriana Fallaci if he was shy, in an interview for *The New Republic*, he replied:

Yes, I am rather. On the other hand, however, I believe I'm fairly well balanced. You see, there are those who describe me as a mysterious, tormented character, and others who see me as a merry guy, smiling, always laughing. Both these images are untrue. I'm neither one nor the other. I'm . . . no, I won't tell you what I am. I'll never tell anyone.

**SELF-IDENTIFICATION CHART**
*YOU ARE AN ANALYZER IF*

| WHEN: | YOU BELIEVE: | BUT OTHERS SAY OR THINK: |
|---|---|---|
| *Conflict Is Brewing* | You have a highly developed awareness when other's verbal reactions are not making sense.<br><br>You know immediately when and how the other is getting caught up in inconsequential, irrelevant issues.<br><br>You can see clearly how to get things back on track before emotional responses start to cloud the issue and things get out of hand | "You don't have to take everything so seriously."<br><br>"Why does everything have to be so exact?"<br><br>"You don't care that I'm so upset about this, do you?!"<br><br>"None of this affects you, does it?" |
| *Conflict Begins* | The solution is not that difficult to grasp and you need to explain it before the other blows everything out of proportion.<br><br>You see the issues clearly and can explain them logically and succinctly so they'll make sense. Silliness and pettiness serve no purpose in trying to resolve a problem and you are put off by an argument presented in this manner.<br><br>You can tell when the other is getting caught up in fuzzy thinking and you try to clarify the position for him/her.<br><br>That emotions should be kept under control and you are baffled when other allows emotions to overtake logic so quickly and completely.<br><br>That when the other is unable to see the problem objectively, he/she tries to lay all the blame on you | "Why does everything have to be so exact and precise for you?"<br><br>"Stop being so detached from everything—this concerns you too!"<br><br>"Why are you so serious—can't you see the funny side of *anything*?"<br><br>"Stop trying to control what I'm saying and how I'm saying it!"<br><br>"Don't be so cold—people do have feelings, you know!"<br><br>"I'm not attacking you personally!" |
| *Conflict Is in Full Swing* | It is important to make other understand the situation objectively—as it really is. | "Stop being so dogmatic!"<br><br>"Why are you always so controlled—for Pete's sake show *some* feeling!" |

| | |
|---|---|
| You must not allow your feelings to get the better of you but must remain calm so as to be able to explain the problem clearly.<br><br>You try to stay patient when other overreacts emotionally.<br><br>Other's hurtful accusations of insensitivity stem from the fact he/she cannot understand the problem in anything other than emotional terms.<br><br>Other intentionally infuriates you with his/her inability to follow what you're saying.<br><br>That when the other introduces all sorts of non-issues that will not change the outcome, you are justified in becoming increasingly annoyed.<br><br>That other's emotional insistence that you are solely to blame when, objectively, you are not, frustrates your patience.<br><br>You keep trying to get other to explain the situation with your clarity and succinctness and know you react badly when they do not | "Stop telling me to pull myself together!"<br>"You're heartless—where's your humanity?!!"<br>"None of this affects you personally at all, does it?"<br>"Why do you always have to be so critical?"<br>"Must you be so sarcastic? And stop talking down to me!"<br>"If you tell me one more time I'm not making sense!"<br>"Do you always have to be so stubborn—you can be wrong sometimes too!"<br>"There's a lot more involved here than just *facts!*"<br>"Please don't repeat the same information over and over."<br>"You're always so inflexible—can't you ever alter your position?" |
| AND AS AN ANALYZER, AS A RESULT, YOU: | AND THEN YOU HEAR: |
| Hit back too hard in attacking any weakness in other's reasoning.<br><br>Become frustrated that other cannot understand what you are saying and you lose patience completely.<br><br>Either turn off until other can regain control and come to his/her senses, or lose control over your own anger, or become depressed at outcome of the conflict and your own inability to keep it under control | "You're just a robot—you haven't a feeling bone in your body!"<br>"Why can't you ever see yourself in the wrong?"<br>"You're not being logical! What you're being is callous!"<br>"Stop feeling sorry for yourself!" |

## SELF-IDENTIFICATION CHART
### YOU ARE AN ELITIST IF

| WHEN: | YOU BELIEVE: | BUT OTHERS SAY OR THINK: |
|---|---|---|
| *Conflict Is Brewing* | You have a highly developed sensitivity to the inappropriateness of others' behavior. You know immediately where the problem lies and how it can be solved. You can easily manipulate others into your way of thinking with intelligence, poise, and skilled persuasion | "Stop giving the impression you're better than everyone else!" "Why do you always think you have the exclusive monopoly on how things should be done?" "Stop being so condescending!" |
| *Conflict Begins* | That if the other is prepared to address the problem intelligently, a satisfactory solution will be reached. You can figure out a realistic solution with the right balance of rational and emotional appeal. It is important that this problem be resolved now. Other is unable to present his/her side of the problem in a coherent manner and you keep trying to get him/her to clarify the matter. That when the other insists on seeing the problem solely from his/her perspective, you are justified in losing patience. That the other is trying to control you when he/she presents a pat solution, expecting you to agree with it, and you resent the attempted manipulation | "I'm sick of your superior attitude!" "Stop being so aloof and removed from this—this is your problem too!" "Why do you always have to act as if you're more intelligent than everyone else—as if you're the only one who can ever come up with some stunning insight!" "Can't you let yourself go and show some earthiness!" "We keep going over the same ground! I'm tired of rehashing the same old stuff!" "You're not hearing what I'm saying—you keep missing things I've said!" "Stop saying you don't understand what I'm trying to say!" "You've always got to be the boss! Can't anyone ever tell *you* what to do?" |

58

| | | |
|---|---|---|
| | That if the other will understand and accept your interpretation of the situation, you can both reach a deeper understanding. | "Why do you always make out I'm stupid when I don't agree with what you say?" |
| | Other is being purposely dense when he/she fails to grasp your line of thought. | "You're always so dominating!" |
| | You will be demeaned if you allow yourself to lose your composure, so you fight to keep control of yourself. | "Why can't you ever accept anyone's suggestions or guidance?" |
| | | "You're incapable of understanding what you've done and the trouble it's caused, aren't you?" |
| | You should try to remain civil and considerate for as long as humanly possible but at times you feel driven to anger by the other's stupidity. | "Stop posturing—it's so artificial. You play the same part and use the same script every time we have this argument!" |
| *Conflict Is in Full Swing* | | "I don't know *what* you're talking about—it doesn't make sense!" |
| | That when you can no longer control your anger, you will be forced to overreact. | "Stop talking down to me! I'm as bright as you are." |
| | That when the other makes you lose your dignity by putting you in the position of having to attack with uncontrolled vehemence, you have a right to show your resentment. | "You're either on the floor or the ceiling—why can't you react normally?" |
| | | "You're always talking about your future—I'm tired of hearing it!" |
| | The problem needs to be resolved here and now or the future consequences will be even more painful. | "You always get so down when we have problems! I can't keep picking you up all the time!" |
| | The tension of a prolonged argument and the seeming impossibility of reaching a solution is deeply depressing | "Why can't I tell you what to do—you're telling me!" |
| | AND AS AN ELITIST, AS A RESULT, YOU: | AND THEN YOU HEAR: |
| | Close in on yourself and cut other out. | "Doesn't anything deflate that massive ego of yours?" |
| | Become depressed that other seems unable to understand your pain, or | "There's no one in your life but you!" |
| | Boil over into anger when other does not even try to relate to your Depression. | "You're always so depressed—I'm sick of trying to cheer *you* up and understand *your* problems all the time!" |

There is, however, that one person who is important to us to whom we *do* want to explain who we are. The Elitist desperately wants that person to understand just what he or she is—and finds it deeply saddening that that person will never really understand how he/she feels.

Elitists know that in conflict they have a hard time relating to that person and getting him or her to see their position. The preceding Self-Identification Chart for the Elitist on pages 58–59 highlights the differences in the way Elitists *think* they are behaving and the way others interpret that behavior.

## MISREADING THE MEANING OF BEHAVIOR

Just as a hologram, when viewed from a different angle or in a different light, reveals a very different picture, so our perception of our own personality and other people's perception of it form two very different pictures.

Things we take for granted about ourselves—because we understand ourselves—are not reflected in our behavior the way we think they are. People read meanings into our words and actions that we do not intend to convey. They *mis*read us. And we, at the same time, are misreading them.

If they are ever going to understand and love us for who we are, it will be by reading the *true* meaning of our words and behavior in the context of our personality type.

And before we can expect the people who are close to us to do that for us, we have to be able to see them as who they really are. We have to understand what they mean *in their terms,* from the perspective of their personality type—*not* in our terms, from our different personality perspective.

### Bodies of Evidence

People feel obliged at one time or another to appear to like, respect, and admire us when in fact they simply cannot stand us.

To do this, they go through a charade of Acceptance, relying on what they're saying to convince us this Acceptance (and even admiration) of us is genuine, heartfelt, and real.

Their bodies, however, may be saying something very different.

Despite what anyone may be *saying* to us, if they display a cluster of any of the following body signals, it is proof positive we are being well and truly rejected:

1.  Their torsos turn away or actually *lean* away from us.
2.  In a sitting position, they stiffen and extend one leg and plant the foot of the other firmly flat on the floor while they are talking.
3.  They tilt one of their shoulders higher than the other.
4.  They either smile too frequently with only their upper teeth showing or freeze a smile or grin into a "war face" for more than 15 seconds.
5.  They shuffle their feet, fidget, play with a prop, or put their reading or regular glasses off and on too frequently.
6.  They steal glances at a clock or a watch.
7.  When we're talking, they bite at their lips or tongue or turn their heads to one side away from us.
8.  Generally, their face muscles remain tight, taut, unrelaxed.
9.  They glance away from us at almost everything else they find more interesting.
10. All their movements are rapid, stiff, and lacking in fluidity.
11. If they return our smile, their eyes are not involved in the emotion.

To believe, without evidence, that we are disliked is paranoia. To have evidence and *proof* we are disliked is not delusion—it is the simple truth.

FOUR

# How to Read
# What People Really Mean

## THE SIGNALS THAT CONVEY OUR TRUE MEANING

What people *really* mean—regardless of what they are actually saying—can be detected in the way they act and react both physically and verbally. Despite the fundamental differences among the four personality types, all four types use the same "signals" to convey their real meanings in what they are doing and saying. These detectable verbal and non-verbal signals come out in exactly the same way in everybody's behavior.

Learning how to read a person's *real* meaning in these signals is the final step in the first of the *3Rs*.

From birth, these signals are sent out loud and clear; yet we haven't been paying enough attention.

For example, if we try to pick up and cuddle a baby who doesn't know us, she sends out unmistakable signals. She draws into herself and clenches her hands, pulls up her legs, and buries her head in her shoulders. Her eyebrows start to knit, her lower lip protrudes, and she may even screw up her eyes and turn her head away. If we persist and lift her up, she stiffens her body, leans precariously back and away from us, and clenches her jaw. She may even push at us with rigid arms. If none of these body language messages gets through to us, the baby then sends out an even more obvious signal: she cries. She doesn't cry gently or softly—she positively bellows. It is almost as if she's saying, "This jerk has missed the subtle signals. Now I have to make it crystal clear that *I don't want to be touched!"*

## PUTTING UP A GOOD FRONT: ADOPTING ROLES AND PLAYING PARTS

The signals we as adults send out about what we really mean may not be as blatantly obvious as a baby's, but they are there to be read just as easily, though in a more discerning way.

The difference between the signals sent out by adults and those broadcast by a baby is that there is no subterfuge about what the baby is trying to convey or the way she conveys it— she expresses *exactly* what she thinks and feels the moment she thinks and feels it, whereas we, as adults, do not, and are constantly constrained from expressing our real thoughts and feelings by the conventions and mores of the society and culture we live in.

We want to weep, but it is considered "unmanly"; we want to act aggressively, but it is considered "unfeminine"; we want to shout and scream in frustration, but it is considered "hysterical."

Just as a baby must, as he or she grows older—as he or she grows into "us"—we learn how to "behave" ourselves. We learn how not to show our true feelings. Instead of weeping openly, we adopt the role of the "strong silent type." Instead of acting aggressively, we adopt the "passive female" role. Instead of yelling in frustration, we become the long-suffering martyr.

In all our adult efforts to "belong" and to gain acceptance, approval, and love, we find ourselves constantly adopting roles and acting out parts, however badly these parts and roles may fit our true personality. Like miscast actors, we find ourselves constantly ill at ease, awkward, and not quite sure of our next line. Rarely, if ever, do we turn in a perfect, convincing performance.

For instance, the non-confrontational Feeler, forced to take a dominating role, may get his lines right for the part, but his delivery of them will always betray a tentativeness and his body language a lack of genuine aggression and control. Similarly, the undemonstrative, systematically minded Analyzer, forced into a caring role, may be able to gush platitudes on cue, but the facial expressions that accompany them will be oddly stiff and her body language will display a distance and lack of warmth.

While we may all be able to live with having to play these parts to cover the inadequacies of our particular personalities in the world at large (in the office or workplace or with people relatively unimportant to us), in private, we all long desperately to be able to "be ourselves" with at least one person who can accept us for what we really are—one person we can trust to understand and cherish those vulnerable parts of us we cannot afford to reveal too openly. And we would gladly reciprocate that trust by accepting unconditionally who that person is in his or her deepest, secret self. Yet, most of the time, we seem incapable of breaking through the facades we have created to protect our tender, inner selves.

We seem incapable because even when we are with someone we trust, from life-long training and almost "force of habit" we find it difficult to express ourselves openly and are *still* constrained and consciously "behaved" in what we say and do. Because we know of no way of seeing beyond this constrained *surface* level of our own and others' behavior, we still rely solely on listening to and believing the messages, the lines, the roles, and the images it conveys. We persist in using this superficial, surface level of behavior to deliver the "behaved" messages of who we feel we should be and what we think we should mean, even when it is vitally important that we convey who we *really* are and what we *really* mean. We do it because we believe—have been taught to believe—there is no other way to do it.

## SUBCONSCIOUS LEAKAGE: WHY WE CAN'T SUPPRESS WHO WE ARE

There is, however, another—deeper—level of communication that we are often unaware we all have, which carries the messages of who we really are and what we really mean. This is the *subconscious level*, which we have not been able to teach "to behave." It is spontaneous, artless, and completely honest. It is that part of us which still has natural, "baby" responses.

And it is so powerful it cannot be quelled. This subconscious level leaks out into our surface behavior, into what we say, the way we say it, and the way our bodies react all the time. No matter how hard we try not to reveal our true thoughts and feelings, we are unable to control the subconscious signals of them that leak (unremittingly) through into our surface behavior.

Like it or not, we are unable to suppress it.

## "I HOPE YOU DIDN'T NOTICE THAT": THE SUBCONSCIOUS "FUMBLE"

A simple yet obvious instance of subconscious signals leaking through to the surface and "tripping up" our conscious verbal and non-verbal behavior sometimes happens when we start to say something we wish we hadn't.

As soon as we become aware of what we're saying and realize the unwanted consequences of completing the idea out loud, we inadvertently send out the following cluster of signals: (1) abruptly stop ourselves in midsentence; (2) shoot up our hand to cover our mouth (to shut off the flow of words); (3) take on a mildly startled *Oops!* look; and (4) quickly examine the expression on the face of the person we're speaking to in order to see if he or she noticed what trouble we're in.

These signals from the subconscious can be detected. They are observable verbal and non-verbal "fumbles," which are not in keeping with the message being conveyed on the conscious, surface level. These individual "fumble" signals group together into *clusters* that carry unmistakable messages.

Even though, at times, we may be aware that everyone sends out these signals and we realize that they carry some type of message, we rarely attach any great significance to them. Instead, we concentrate on and accept only what people want us to hear and see, just as, in turn, we hope they will only concentrate on and accept what we want them to see and hear. We do not want them to pick up on the clusters of subconscious signals we make all the time, which could reveal exactly what we really think—despite what we're saying.

## "Believe Me, I'm Telling the Truth": How the Truth Leaks Out

If we are to understand what people *really* mean by the things they say and do, this subconscious leakage is the very level of communication we must learn to read. These clusters of signals are the language of the innermost self, openly revealing exactly what it means.

Consider, for example, the following clusters of signals sent out by a man who is suspected by his wife of being unfaithful.

Earlier in the evening he has called to tell her he will have to work late yet again, and at 3:00 A.M. he arrives home looking appropriately exhausted. Yet, this evening, she has even more than her usual uneasy feeling about him and decides, for the first time, to confront him with her suspicions.

As she talks, he folds his arms across his chest and turns side on to her. He does not hear her out. His reaction to her accusation is one of anger. He plants his hands on his hips and turns to face her. He glares at her, purses his lips, looks her straight in the eye without blinking, clears his throat, and says, "That's ridiculous! Why would anyone in my position want to play around with a younger woman? He'd have to be crazy!" Then, getting a grip on himself, he rubs at his nose and smiles reassuringly at her. He takes her in his arms, saying gently, "Honest to God, darling, I'd never, ever do anything like that, really." He laughs. "It was just that that frustrating managing director personally asked me to do a gargantuan-sized rush job. My report on it has to be at the Rome office by 5:00 A.M. their time, this morning. Truthfully, I just managed to fax it off before I left the office twenty minutes ago."

And she believes him.

She believes him because she is hearing only the superficial meaning of his words and reacting only to his contrived behavior. She is not reading and interpreting the clusters of subconscious signals leaking out into all his speech and behavior patterns.

She is taken in by his role as the hardworking, faithful husband, and by the fact that she wants to believe him. Yet, if she had been able to read what he *really* meant by the things he did and said in this short exchange, she would have picked up at least thirteen body language and seventeen verbal signals that are at complete odds with the story he is trying to sell and at complete odds with the role he is trying to play.

### Body Language Signals: How the Subconscious Leaks Out into What We Do and the Way We Do It

His *body language signals* alone, before he even says a word, should have alerted her to the gulf between what he says and what he really means. For example, when she confronts him with her suspicions, he crosses his arms over his chest, signaling that he is closing himself off from her. He is not "open" to listening to her concerns, but is intent on protecting and defending himself from attack. With his body turned away from her he is signaling his subconscious attempt to evade the issue, hoping it will slide past him. He has already decided not to face the problem head-on.

At the point in the story where he has decided he must take control in order to convince her and throw her off with his anger, his hands go to his hips, with his fingers pointing down to his genital area. This is an obvious male aggressive pose signal he adopts instinctively to dominate her.

These gross body movements are easy to notice. They are as obvious as the physical reactions of the baby who does not want to be picked up by the stranger. Whether or not the husband knows it, his true, subconscious message is coming through loud and clear.

And there are even more subtle physical movements and gestures in this exchange. When he first hears her accusation, the husband's fear of discovery has caused a physical reaction that affects the color of his skin. The sides of his face redden slightly and the skin on his neck shows a reddish blotching.

His wife probably did not attach any significance to the fact that he rubs at his nose at the point in the exchange where he has decided to calm himself down and try another approach; but she should have. In high stress, the erectile tissues of the nasal passages become engorged with blood, causing the nose to become highly sensitive. The "Pinocchio

Syndrome" signal of rubbing, stroking, or pulling at the nose
to alleviate stress, when read in a cluster of signals, is a sure
sign of lying.

---

### The "Pinocchio Syndrome"

Pinocchio's nose gave him away when he lied.

Our noses give us away when we lie.   It is not that, like Pinocchio, our noses grow a little with each lie, but that our noses
actually *tickle* a little with each lie. And, without realizing it, we
then frequently touch, pull, or tug on the lower part to alleviate
that tickle.

This irritating "tickling" sensation occurs when the erectile tissues around the nasal passages engorge with blood in response
to emotional and mental stress.

As few of us can lie without experiencing some degree of
stress (over the fear of being found out, or guilt over the thing
we're lying about, or simple anxiety at the credibility of the unlikely story we're spinning), our noses start prickling spontaneously. Then, while we speak, we brush at them or even actually
pinch the nostrils closed to relieve the sensation.

So, when it comes to lying, the creator of the Pinocchio story
had it right—the nose knows.

---

In these few instances, the body language signals alone
thrown up in this scenario are examples of the types of physical behavior that illustrate graphically what a person is really
thinking and feeling—regardless of what is being said.

And there are other signals and reasons for them.

There is a reason for every movement, gesture, and expression a person makes, intentional or not. In stress, especially,
the body needs to dissipate energy with movement, and those
movements subconsciously signal—despite the actors'
"roles" and "lines"—what is really going on in the mind of
the real person behind them.

Sometimes the meanings of these non-verbal signals are
clear and obvious; at other times they appear ambiguous,
puzzling, even totally incomprehensible. Yet even though one
apparently innocuous signal may not convey any particular

meaning, several signals read together as a "cluster" do form a definite pattern and convey a clear message.

A list of body language signals and their meanings appears in the Appendix.

### VERBAL SIGNALS: HOW THE SUBCONSCIOUS LEAKS OUT INTO WHAT WE SAY AND THE WAY WE SAY IT

The message becomes even clearer when the non-verbal, body language signals form clusters along with the *verbal signals*. Verbal and non-verbal signals work in tandem. They complement and reinforce each other. The combined subconscious leakage into *what* a person says, *how* he or she says it, and *the way* his or her body reacts produces a richness of clusters of verbal and non-verbal language that delivers the true message of what that person means with unconscious eloquence.

Even though we believe we have total control over what we say—and we tend to use speech as the primary mask to convey our chosen image in our role playing—the subconscious truth of what we really mean still leaks through.

The Freudian slip is the most obvious: for example, the cheating husband's inadvertent reference to "a younger woman" when his wife has made no mention of the age of a possible lover at all, is an allusion that—had the husband had conscious control of what he was saying—he would never have used.

Similarly, more subtle but nevertheless obvious leaks are revealed in the types of phrases and expressions he uses. For example, he employs the expression "play around." He does not think of himself as doing anything so vile as "committing adultery," so he minimizes his unfaithfulness in his own mind into "playing around." His use of the expression "do anything like that" is also self-revealing: anything like "playing around" is still "playing around"—is in fact adultery.

Less obvious, but just as telling, subconscious leaks can be detected in the choice of words used. Her husband's use of the word "gargantuan" may momentarily strike his wife as nothing more than slightly odd; but when in stress, people tend to draw on a vocabulary outside their normal range, and often use (and misuse) esoteric words they think will strengthen the impact of what they're saying to make it more credible.

The husband's use of the adjective "frustrating" to describe his managing director is an example of the subconscious leaking out oblique references to its *own* state of mind. The theme of frustration probably describes not the husband's relationship with his managing director, but the husband's feelings in his relationship with his wife. Rather than openly using the word "frustrated" to explain his behavior—since he intends to deny his behavior anyway—his subconscious shifts it into a less provocative, unconfrontational context.

More prosaically, what a person says also includes, of course, the outright lie. The husband's story about his report having to be in Rome "by 5:00 A.M. their time, this morning" is obvious rubbish once you look beyond the glibness of his delivery. As the time zone for Italy has to be at least six hours ahead of U.S. Eastern Standard Time, he would have had to fax the report by 11:00 P.M. at night at the latest, not twenty minutes before he got home at 3:00 A.M.

Further, when *what* is said is additionally combined with *how* it is said, the real message becomes even easier to read.

An abrupt midsentence cutoff often occurs when the speaker realizes he doesn't have total control over what he's saying, or he may merely pause, subconsciously using a stalling tactic to buy time by uttering a few "Umm's" and "Ah's," and then confidently continuing with what he hopes is an acceptable ending to the sentence.

Or, it might be even subtler still: the amateur adulterer who clears his throat before launching into his alibi is like the speaker who coughs or clears his throat before stepping up to the podium. He wants his intended message to come through loud and clear: he's focused his thoughts, he's decided on the image he wants to project, he's determined to convince his audience: "Cough, cough . . . I'm ready, here it comes!"

How what is being said is also strongly influenced by changes in the *volume*, *rate*, *pitch*, and *tone* of the voice. There is as much subconscious information being leaked through these outlets as there is in any of the others previously discussed. A person is rarely conscious, until it is too late, that she has started to speak more softly or more slowly, or even louder or more quickly, than she normally does. She is frequently unaware that the pitch of her voice can change because of what she is really thinking and feeling.

A list of verbal signals and their meanings appears in the Appendix.

## Everyday Lie Detecting: Clusters of Verbal and Physical Signals

These few explanations of lie detecting, which reveal what a person is secretly thinking—no matter what he or she may be trying to convey on a superficial level—are examples of the sort of verbal signals and clusters that have to be picked up on and read.

When verbal signals are combined with non-verbal signals and grouped into clusters, the subconscious message sent out to us is unmistakable.

The scenario of the unfaithful husband, being purposely and all too consciously deceptive, illustrates that even when what a person says is the exact opposite of what he or she really thinks and means, the *real* subconscious message can be read with unmistakable clarity. When the difference between what someone is thinking and saying is less polarized, the detectable signals can still be read with equal clarity. None of us can staunch the leakage of these signals into our conscious behavior. We send them out, in some way or other, in every waking moment of our lives.

### The Uneasy Feeling of Missing Something: The Importance of Reading the Real Message

All these illustrations of verbal and physical behavior are familiar. We see and hear them—and others like them—all the time. While there are moments when we do realize the significance of some of these subconscious signals and respond to them, there are others when we sense that appearance and reality may be very different. We just get an uneasy feeling that we are missing something—but don't quite know what. So often, talking with or just being with someone, we have a sense that there is an undercurrent of something that needs to come to the surface. We realize that whatever it is that we can't quite put our finger on is important, maybe even crucial, to our relationship with that person; but as we don't know exactly what it is, we don't know how to respond.

Since we are overlooking almost all of the vitally important *real* information about one other that our subconscious selves are so busy trying to communicate, it's not surprising that we seem incapable of breaking through one another's facades to reach that genuine understanding we long for. But all the signals being sent from behind that facade are there to be seen and heard by anyone who cares to read them.

For so long we have taken it for granted that the *only* level of communication is the superficial level of what is being intentionally said and done; we have been blind and deaf to the abundant wealth of unintentional information flowing all around us.

Yet, all that is required to tap into this information and read it is the ability to be aware of what is really happening: to look and *see,* to listen and *hear.*

### Rules for Reading Behavior Signals

Observe and concentrate.

Look and *see.*

Listen and *hear.*

Never *assume* anyone's projected image is his or her real image.

Identify their personality type.

Establish their *normal* physical and verbal behavior patterns
and note *variations* from that norm.

Be *aware* of subconscious leaks into their conscious behavior.

Note that *verbal* and *non-verbal signals* work in tandem.

Remember that one signal standing alone means nothing. Signals must *cluster* before a conclusion can be drawn.

# PART TWO

# "READ
AND
RESPOND"

# FIVE

# Acceptance and Rejection

## "WHY DO WE ALWAYS HAVE THE SAME ARGUMENT OVER AND OVER?": THE NATURE OF CONFLICT

Pivotal to all human behavior—whatever our personality type—is the twin notion of *Acceptance* and *Rejection*.

To put it simply: we just plain like being *accepted*. It puts us in a good mood and arouses positive thoughts and feelings. We feel well-disposed toward the persons accepting us and react well to them.

On the other hand, once someone *rejects* us—especially someone who is important to us—we experience all sorts of negative thoughts and feelings, find ourselves in a bad mood, and start reacting badly toward him or her.

In all our close relationships, whether with our parents, children, lovers, spouses, or friends, one of us invariably does or says something that irks the other. One of us then objects and the other takes offense. We both feel rejected and we argue.

Depending on our respective personality types, we fall into

particular, almost ritualistic, patterns of conflict that we seem doomed to repeat over and over.

The second of the *3Rs, Respond,* is concerned with understanding why and how this happens, and how to go about stopping it from ever happening again.

## DRIVING EACH OTHER CRAZY: MUTUAL REJECTION

When things are going well on both sides—when we are in Mutual Acceptance of each other and especially of our personality differences—we tend to overlook each other's bad points because the good points are so appealing to us.

For example, the fact that he (your Feeler) takes forever just to decide where he wants to go for dinner seems unimportant when you realize he's chosen somewhere he knows you like more than he does. The fact that she (your Driver) snaps at your closest friends every time they disagree with you seems trifling when you realize that, to her mind, you are always right.

Yet there are times when we find it more and more difficult to overlook the other person's bad points or put a good gloss on them. His inability to make up his mind quickly and decisively about *anything* can so infuriate you, you begin to reject everything about him. Her inability to stop interrupting with her unwanted opinions can so frustrate you, you begin to disapprove of everything about her.

You then begin to drive each other crazy; and if neither of you is able to reverse the process, what was once Mutual Acceptance, approval, and love can turn into mutual rejection, disapproval, and deep resentment. And *continued* Mutual Rejection can turn into open animosity, even hate.

Yet it is the acceptance, indeed approval, of those—now so repelling—differences between two people's personalities that may have drawn them to each other in the first place.

For example, put the mutually appealing personalities of

the Feeler and the Driver together, and the mesh can be so perfect they seem made for each other. But add mutual irritation and stress to the fusion, and this once perfect pair can become the cruelest combination for mutual destruction.

The compassionate Feeler, who is the warmest, most loving, thoughtful, and considerate of people when loved and accepted, can, if continually rejected, eventually be turned into the coldest, most withdrawn, stubborn, and selfish of people. And the outgoing Driver, who is protective, vibrant, and so expressively loving when accepted, can, if continually rejected, become the most unforgiving, belligerent tyrant who ever drew breath.

The saddest part of all this is that once this intensification of rejection has begun, it seems to these two people that there is no way of halting an apparently inevitable headlong rush toward break-up; or, in the case of marriage, separation, divorce, and bitter regrets.

## WHEN WE JUST WON'T GIVE IN: THE INTENSIFICATION OF REJECTION

This serial progression toward total failure of a relationship *can* be stopped, simply by recognizing what is happening and knowing what to do about it. The intensification of rejection can be read and responded to in such a way that it is halted and turned back into Acceptance, long before it reaches the point of mutual destruction.

In order to put a stop to the intensification process, we have to realize just what we are doing subconsciously when we feel rejected.

Because we don't like the negative thoughts and emotions aroused in us when someone rejects us, we struggle to get them to accept us again. It seems to us that the simplest way of doing this is either: to give in to the person who is rejecting us by agreeing with them; or, to get them to agree with us.

When someone rejects us over something relatively minor (such as our choice of a movie or where we should go to eat out), most of us opt for the first course and simply give in— "Okay, that's fine with me"—because it prevents an inevitable argument, and because what we wanted was not that important anyway.

The rejection has been nipped in the bud and has not been allowed to intensify.

But there are times when what we want *is* important and we refuse just to give in. Further, we don't want the other person just to agree with us because it isn't important to them; we want them to agree with us because what we want is *right.*

Unfortunately, at these times, "they" usually feel the same way. And the more intensely we reject them, the more strongly they reject us.

So we fight. We twist ourselves in and out of all sorts of mental contortions and painful emotions trying to convince the other to accept our point of view, at the same time trying to fend off and not be hurt by the assault of someone trying to convince us of theirs.

## TACTICAL SELF-PROTECTION AND MANIPULATION: THE FOUR MOODS OF REJECTION

In our struggle to get the other person to see, and accept, our own point of view, we battle back and forth—each of us using the tried-and-true methods of "persuasion" that have worked for us in the past. In doing this, we go through certain well-defined stages called *Moods.*

These four *Moods of Rejection* we experience are known as: DENIAL, ANGER, DEPRESSION, BARGAINING.

Often we pass through them so quickly we are unaware ourselves that they are even there. Even when we *are* aware that we are in one or more of these moods, we are not fully aware of how they are affecting us.

Yet, whether or not we know it, these moods are the subconscious mechanisms that allow us to deal with the thoughts and emotions we experience in being rejected; and, at the same time manipulate the other person into accepting our position.

Each of these moods has its own separate and distinct set of tactics, designed to enable us to protect ourselves and our position, while allowing us to force our adversary to capitulate and accept our terms. In the to and fro of any conflict we subconsciously draw on the tactical advantages peculiar to each mood that give us the greatest leverage over our opponent.

Whatever the cause of our argument, whatever the negative thoughts and feelings aroused in us, whatever our personality type, we *all* go through one or more of these four moods in our attempts to handle rejection.

Depending on our particular personality type, we use this limited number of moods with greater or lesser skill, with varying degrees of intensity, and in a different order of priority.

### The Course of Jealousy: An Example of Moods in Action

Consider, for example, just one of the complex reactions to rejection we experience: that of the feeling of jealousy that arises when we think we are being passed over in favor of someone else.

Bonny, a twenty-four-year-old computer programmer from Florida, was forced to deal with emotions of fear, envy, resentment, hatred, frustration, dejection, and self-pity when she discovered that her boyfriend was taking computer lessons from her best friend.

Bonny knew that her boyfriend, Len, wanted to learn how

to use a computer, so she offered to teach him. For some reason she didn't understand, he seemed reluctant to accept her offer, so she let the matter drop. Then she found out that her best friend was teaching him. She was deeply hurt and a feeling of jealousy overwhelmed her.

At first, in the Mood of Denial, she tried to put the whole thing out of her mind. She didn't even mention to Len that she'd heard he was taking lessons from her friend; she pretended nothing had happened and forced herself to act "normally" toward both him and her best friend.

However, there came a point when she could no longer keep her emotions bottled up and they escaped in a jealous rage in the Mood of Anger. She confronted Len and accused him of being attracted to her friend, of being underhanded and going behind her back. She attacked her friend for "stealing" her boyfriend, and she vented her anger at anything and everything that seemed to be against her.

Len was taken aback. When he couldn't get a word in edgewise to explain why he had asked her friend, instead of her, to teach him, he simply walked out.

Left alone, Bonny then turned her anger in on herself and collapsed into the Mood of Depression. She was consumed by feelings of self-pity over her own inadequacies and frustration at her inability to handle the situation properly.

When she eventually pulled herself together and realized she might have done irreparable damage by the things she had said to Len, she began to think she might be able to turn his rejection back into acceptance and, in a Mood of Bargaining, worked out how she could "cut some sort of deal" for herself. She considered apologizing and promising never to accuse him of anything like that again. She even thought of buying him a present to soften him up. Then she settled on the idea of inviting him over for a romantic evening so she could use all her powers of sexual persuasion to win him back and apologize properly.

However, things didn't work out quite the way she'd planned because Len was himself going through all the moods and was still firmly entrenched in his own Mood of Anger.

Just as Bonny had to deal with her thoughts and feelings of jealousy in these four moods, we all deal with *any* form of rejection by subconsciously shifting in and out of Denial, Anger, Depression, and Bargaining.

From the most fleeting instances of rejection (our date not liking our choice of movie), to the most frustrating (our spouse detesting our best friend), to the shattering (the decision to end a twenty-four-year relationship), to the ultimate (the very process of death itself), we all suffer through one or more of these moods in our attempts to handle our distress.

If we are not in acceptance, we are in rejection, and we find ourselves acting and reacting—emotionally and rationally—in one of these four moods.

Depending on the intensity and protraction of the rejection, we draw on some or all of the range of tactics for self-protection and manipulation peculiar to each mood, subconsciously slipping in and out of each as we battle to reach Acceptance.

## "IF YOU'D JUST SEE THINGS MY WAY . . .": EFFORTS AT "MOOD BONDING"

Our need and desire to be accepted are so powerful that even while we are actively rejecting some aspect of the person we are in conflict with, ironically, we are still (like Bonny) using each of these moods as an attempt to *bond* with that person.

If their acceptance were not so important to us we would not be struggling our way through these moods, we would be merely *indifferent* to what they think of us. Instead, we are putting ourselves through the emotional and mental turmoil of these moods in an appeal for their approval by saying, in effect: "If you'll just see things my way, you'll see I'm not a bad person, and then you can stop rejecting me and love me again!"

Yet we never seem to be able to say this *directly* to each other.

Instead, we hint at it, we imply it, burying our appeal for understanding in so much verbiage it rarely comes through loud and clear.

## THE SPECIFIC MEANING HIDDEN IN OUR WORDS: OUR THEME

But, if we know how to listen, it is there—always—in our *theme.*

The exact meaning of what we are really trying to say— what we want the other person to accept—is always contained in this theme.

Our theme is not only the opinion or line of thought we are voicing, but also the *implied, unspoken appeal for acceptance of our worth and value as a human being* that we are trying to convey through that opinion.

And that unspoken appeal for acknowledgment of our worth is by far the more important part of our theme.

Take, for example, a squabble over whether or not the two of you should go out or stay in for the evening: One of you wants to go out, and says, "But we haven't been out for ages and *you know how much I love going for a walk in the evenings!*"

The other says, "I just don't feel up to it this evening, *can't you see I'm exhausted?*"

The respective themes are: "I want to go out" and "I don't want to go out," *together with* the unspoken, implied appeal behind those opposing stances: "Please acknowledge my importance to you. Please value who I am and understand that I need you to think of me."

Our theme is the essence of what we are getting at. Because it is so important to us to have this theme understood and accepted, it motivates us to keep arguing, to refuse to give up or give in.

To our minds, it is inextricably tied up with who and what we are, with our worth and value as a human being. We sense that once this theme is accepted, *we* shall have been accepted and validated as who and what we are. We believe that the person we are struggling so desperately to bond with cannot really love us unless and until he or she understands and accept this theme.

Whatever our theme, we always *repeat* it throughout a conversation or argument. We may or may not repeat it in the exact same words, but its meaning returns over and over in one way or another until it is accepted.

## "LISTEN TO WHAT I'M TRYING TO TELL YOU": USING MOODS TO GET OUR THEME ACROSS

Each mood enables us to repeat our theme in a different way: in the Mood of Anger, we demand that our theme be met; in the Mood of Depression, we plead for it to be addressed; in the Mood of Bargaining, we cajole the other person into acceptance of it.

In our efforts to force a bond and understanding of our real meaning, we set about manipulating the other person into accepting us. Each mood affords us a different set of tactics for taking control and influencing the outcome of conflict in our favor.

We use *Anger* to dominate and control other people and the direction of the conflict we are purposely trying to generate. We try to force acceptance of our theme through power. Being in no mood to consider their point of view, all we want to do is vent our thoughts and feelings in the most overpowering and aggressive way possible. Our Anger thrives on fric-

tion and is fueled and fed by resistance. Resistance to it justi-
fies our getting angrier and angrier in response, and allows
us to take a more and more extreme and dominating position.

In *Depression,* we turn the anger in on ourselves and let it
feed away at us. We feel sorry for ourselves—and the more
we attack ourselves, the sadder we become. We display our
Depression in an attempt to get the other person to feel sorry
for us and acknowledge our theme. We implore them to
soothe and alleviate our sadness, and to understand and accept the reasons for it.

We use *Bargaining* to cajole the other person into acceptance of our theme. We pretend to see the other person's
point of view in order to get something for ourselves, and
concede something in their favor to wangle something
greater in return. We try to maneuver them into acceptance
of us through our mock acceptance of them.

In *Denial,* we try to avoid the issue. We cannot face the
rejection or come to terms with it. We either deny the truth
to ourselves; or deny the truth to others.

The first is a form of self-delusion and self-deception. We
virtually hypnotize ourselves into ignoring the existence of
another's position and even the reality of our own situation.
We find the truth too distressing to face and Denial stops us
having to come to terms with it. We refuse even to consider
the possibility that we could be wrong. We will not accept
what the other person is saying. In effect, we are saying to
*ourselves,* "I can't believe that!"

The second is pure deception or lying. We refuse to admit
to others that we know the truth, so we do and say things—
which we know are not true—in order to deceive the other
person. We persist in saying to *them,* "I don't believe that!"

In both forms of Denial we try, through insistence that
something is not happening, to persuade the other person to
accept our point of view.

While we are caught up in these four moods, the person we are trying to bond with—while adamantly rejecting us—is just as paradoxically and just as desperately trying to get us to accept *their* theme by using the same four moods.

In our continuing rejection of each other—in our failure to give each other the acceptance, approval, and respect we both want so badly—we push each other, and ourselves, in, out and through the chaos of Denial, Anger, Depression, and Bargaining.

## "Hey, I'm Important Too!": The Moods at Work

John, a representative for a paper distributor, who is on the road selling two months out of three, values every moment he spends at home with his family. At his wits' end over how to stop the annual six-week invasion of his wife's family into his home, and deeply depressed at the way he and his wife, Lucy, both seem to get stuck in same old groove every time they even try to discuss the problem, John related the following typical exchange they have each year.

Read the left-hand column through first to get the gist of their argument. Then read each paragraph of the dispute separately, continuing across into the right-hand column to see how each of them is—unknowingly—using the tactics of the various moods to manipulate the other into Acceptance of their respective *themes*.

**JOHN:**

"Please, dear, we have to discuss things. This is the third year in a row your brother and his family have come to spend Thanksgiving and ended up staying on for the full three weeks of their vacation.

He is approaching the problem in *Bargaining:* by being overly polite and gracious in order to get her to accept his view that three weeks is too long to put up with her relatives.

"It's a little tough on me because with all the out-of-state traveling I do, I'm tired when I get home and I need to relax with just my family.

"You know I work hard. You know I'm tired when I get back and it takes me a day just to recuperate."

His theme is emerging in *Depression.*

He is *Bargaining* when he says, "I work hard," because he expects her to read in "for you and our kids," and he is appealing for something in return for that. His continued reference to his tiredness emphasizes his point with a hint of *Depression.* He is trying to bond with her and manipulate her into acceptance of his position.

"I know, you love your brother and his family—they're nice people—but can't we just have them stay a couple of days and then go home?

"You're so good the way you treat them and do everything for them. I know you love them but . . ."

He is couching his suggested solution in the *Bargaining* tactics of flattery and concession to her position.

While cajoling her with *Bargaining,* he is also trying to repeat his *theme:* "But . . . can't your love for me and what I want and need take precedence over your brother and his needs?"

**Lucy:**

"I love my brother! You're going to have to understand I miss him when he's not here and he misses me.

"Besides, with you on the road so much and the kids away at school all day, I get lonely here. Having them all in the house for three weeks is great for me.

"But if you want to change the arrangement, you can talk to him if you like—I don't want to hurt his feelings."

Locked in *Denial,* she simply ignores his theme and his bonding attempts. She is in total rejection of him and his position.

Her *theme* emerges in *Depression:* "You leave me alone and lonely," and in *Bargaining* by hinting, "so don't I deserve some company?"

She does an about-face out of *Denial* and shifts into *Bargaining,* conceding that he has a point, and offers a deal.

"No. On second thought I don't want you to do that. You're so blunt, you'll offend him."

Fearing she will lose out on the deal, she swings back into rejection, using *Denial* of her husband's personality.

JOHN:

"Here we go again! They were here for three weeks at Thanksgiving, and now it's only the beginning of June—my heavy period for work—and they're back again!

"Don't I count for anything around here?

"Didn't you hear me last time? Don't you get it? I'm not getting through to you at all, am I?"

The previous rejection is repeated in terms of unveiled *Anger.*
[There is the danger of a pattern being set up and the problem becoming cyclic.]

His *theme* of "why does your brother have first call on your attention—what about me?" is repeated in *Anger* and *Depression.*

He uses *Anger* to vent his frustration at having his *theme* ignored.

LUCY:

"You don't care about me or my family!

"All you care about is you and how tired you are at that stupid job you've got.

"Why don't you quit and get a nine to five job like everybody else?

"I hate your job and how tired it makes you!"

She is restating her theme bluntly in *Anger* and *Depression.*

Still in *Denial,* she is refusing to acknowledge there is a problem and ignores his *Depression* of the previous argument.

In her *Anger,* she is lashing out at an irrelevant issue.

Her *theme*—"So you never have time for me"—is repeated obliquely in terms of *Anger.*

JOHN:

"Okay. Good. Then maybe I'll just get out and find someone who doesn't hate me or my job! And doesn't fill my house with their damned freeloading family!"

Set in *Denial,* he is ignoring her *theme* and in *Anger* attacks her, her family, and the situation. His threat is repeating his *theme* that he wants someone who will value him.

## TURNING BACK THE TIDE: RESPONDING TO THESE MOODS

We are all familiar with the sense of increasing frustration being experienced by this couple as they battle through the moods, each trying to make the other understand what they are really getting at.

Yet this painfully chaotic process can be halted simply by addressing and satisfying the particular *theme* being expressed through the use of each of these moods.

Once we feel that our emotional and rational self has been given the attention and respect we deserve, and that our right to react the way we do is acknowledged as being justified, we willingly let ourselves drift out of the particular mood we have dug our heels into.

Defused and appeased, we are then more receptive to giving our opponent the same consideration that has been given to us. We are getting closer to accepting each other again.

For example, even two strangers who are almost involved in an auto collision and come to a screeching halt half an inch from each other are thrown into moods. If they both explode into the Mood of Anger and leap from their cars, ready to rip each other limb from limb, the ensuing confrontation can be devastating.

However, if one of the motorists gets out of his car and exclaims: "Hell, I'm sorry. That was my fault. Are you okay?" the fury of the other driver is immediately defused. She no longer feels an overwhelming urge to pummel the offending driver into oblivion. Her right to her feeling of anger has been acknowledged as being justified. She already feels somewhat appeased. Rather than yelling and cursing violently at top volume, she merely vents her annoyance in grumbling.

She might even be ready to listen to the other driver's explanation for what he did, which—who knows?—might even be justified.

Just as easily as the Anger of the now placated driver was defused through acceptance of her position, Anger can become intensified. If met with rejection, it will grow more and more destructive.

Anger is not the only mood that can be handled the right way or the wrong way. We can *respond* to each of the Moods of Rejection in such a way as to lead anyone back into Acceptance.

## RITUALISTIC PATTERNS OF CONFLICT: BREAKING THE CYCLE

In our daily relationships with people who are not strangers, we constantly find ourselves intensifying, rather than defusing, each other's moods by responding to their mood with one of our own, and simply ignoring their themes.

Depending on our respective personality types, we both trap ourselves in almost ritualistic patterns of conflict and argument, triggering the same reactions over and over. We get caught up in a mutually destructive pattern that we seem doomed to repeat ad infinitum.

Neither of us appears able to break the inevitable sequence in and out of Denial, Anger, Depression, and Bargaining to cut through—into accepting what we are really trying to get each other to understand.

But it can be done. Each of us can be drawn through our Moods of Rejection into Acceptance of each other again. Since all we are asking for, anyway, is that the other person accept and respect who and what we are—acknowledge our value and worth, to them—all we have to do is address the theme as it emerges in each of these moods.

Just as the originally furious motorist, once defused, is prepared at least to listen to the other driver's explanation, our opponent in conflict—once defused and appeased in each of his moods—is willing, indeed *wants*, in turn, to address our needs.

It is simply a matter of reading how a person is using each of the Moods of Rejection to get you to meet his or her theme; and responding to each mood so as to guide that person, slowly but surely, through into Acceptance.

## Mutual Acceptance: How to Achieve It

Like navigators leading someone who is important to us toward a destination we both want to reach, we have to recognize the markers of the moods that help us locate the best and safest route to bring the person we care for, and ourselves, safely back home into Mutual Acceptance.

The steps to achieving this goal are:

1. Neutralize our own moods.
2. *Read* their theme and the moods they are using to deliver it in.
3. *Respond* to their theme in each of their moods so as to appease and defuse that mood; address and satisfy their theme; and guide them through into Acceptance.
4. Reach Mutual Acceptance through *Reciprocation.*

This may sound manipulative and calculating, and it is. But essentially it is a manipulation of *ourselves* into an understanding of the other person's needs. And then, through our understanding and acknowledgment of those needs, getting the person to meet and satisfy *our* needs.

### Decisions, Decisions . . .

We have all seen the following familiar scene in a restaurant:

A young couple settle themselves at a table and pick up their menus. He skims through the listings and, quickly seeing what he wants, makes his decision and closes the menu, ready for some conversation. He is a *Driver*.

She, on the other hand, studies each item, flipping back and forth as she carefully considers everything on offer. She is a *Feeler*.

He starts fidgeting. Aware of his impatience, she looks up from her menu and smiles, announcing her choice tentatively.

Relieved, he takes her menu, closes it, and starts talking about something else.

However, not being totally satisfied, she only half listens and keeps glancing at the closed menu on the table, becoming more and more unhappy at her rushed decision.

He becomes irritated with her. In turn, she grows even less attentive and more unhappy.

They start a scene—a rerun of the same old argument.

"The same old argument" is about the infuriating and frustrating way the other makes decisions, from something as trivial as the purchase of groceries to something as critical as the purchase of a new home—and everything in between.

Each of them thinks the other should make a decision his or her way—the "correct" way. Neither of them realizes that because of their different personalities, neither of them can do this.

- *Feelers* need to consider *all* the ramifications of any decision slowly and carefully. They feel bound to explore all the alternatives, then compare and contrast them, gradually narrowing down the options, until they can make a thoroughly considered choice.
- *Drivers,* on the other hand, scan the options quickly, lighting rapidly on their selection. Then, having made the "right" choice, they are no longer interested in alternatives. Their minds are made up and that's that.
- *Analyzers* weigh what is right and wrong for them in an orderly, very structured fashion, taking into account the purpose of the choice, and then select the option that makes the most "sense" in the circumstances.
- *Elitists* go through a version of all the above ways of making a decision, but invariably choose an option that is non-standard, definitely not "ordinary" or "common," but which is "appropriate" to their standing.

Each type agrees on only one thing about the way the others make decisions: that it is alien, irksome, and thoroughly frustrating.

But, like the personality types themselves, this cannot be changed. And if two people are to avoid not just a single public scene in a restaurant but a series of private ones in a relationship, the types must be allowed to make their own decisions their own way—and given all the time they need to reach them.

# SIX

# How to Read Mood Language

## "I'M TRYING TO TELL YOU WHAT I WANT": THE MESSAGE OF MOODS

We have all been "reading" the language of each other's moods all our lives.

Any child knows that when his mother starts glaring at him and her voice begins to rise, he'd better get his alibi right because she's in a Mood of Anger. However, he may not be able to read that she is merely faking that mood to control his wayward behavior. If he could read what she *really* means, he'd be able to defuse her rejection of him almost instantaneously.

Similarly, two people who love each other, but who keep arguing, may be aware that they are constantly pushing each other into and through Denial, Anger, Depression, and Bargaining. Yet they are frustratingly unable to pinpoint what it is they are *really* trying to say to each other through these moods, and consequently never seem able to respond to each other's needs.

Before any of us can begin to respond to each other's real

needs, we have to be able to read each other's Mood Language accurately. This is because Mood Language is what we all use to convey what we really mean and what we really want from each other.

## THE WHAT AND HOW OF MOOD LANGUAGE

This Mood Language is expressed both *verbally* and *non-verbally.*

The real meaning of what a person is trying to say can only be clearly read in the full context of: *what* they express verbally; and *how* they express it verbally, vocally, and physically.

Our mental and emotional responses to the Moods of both Acceptance and Rejection are accompanied by physical changes in our bodies, which have a pronounced effect on the way we express ourselves in each of our moods. Our behavior varies in distinct ways as we experience alterations in our heart rate, respiratory activity, muscle tone, and even the size of our blood vessels with each mood change.

These combined mental, emotional, and physical reactions produce a "truth" that cannot be suppressed, a "truth" that leaks out into everything we say and do, a "truth" that is expressed in a form we may never have understood before or even known was there: Mood Language.

Mood Language is not difficult to read. We all do it instinctively anyway in a hit-or-miss fashion, without realizing it. However, in order to read a person's real meaning all the time, we have to learn to understand, not randomly but *systematically,* what it is they are trying to tell us.

We must learn to look and *see,* listen and *hear,* sense and *deeply understand.*

We must learn their Mood Language.

## What to See, Hear, and Sense: General Guidelines

The following general guidelines list the six things you must see, hear, and sense in order to read Mood Language.

If you keep these specific points in mind every time you have a conversation with anyone, you will become acutely aware of the eloquence of Mood Language and all the meanings you may have been missing.

Your skill at reading this language will increase as you become more and more aware of the type of information you are taking in. You will suddenly realize that you are making sense of—and understanding—the real meaning of what people are saying to you.

### 1. Any variation from the norm

As Mood Language is expressed through variations from a person's "normal" physical and verbal behavior, you must first establish what their normal physical and verbal behavior is.

For example, no mood significance should be read into the behavior of someone who normally slouches when he walks, who slumps comfortably and naturally into a chair, and who usually looks you straight in the eye when he talks to you in a soft, slow, but boring voice, without using gestures to enhance what he's saying.

However, if this same person pulls his shoulders back, sits up straight in a chair, starts gesticulating emphatically, and will not look directly at you as his voice rises and his speech becomes vigorous, then you should be reading his Mood Language with great attention—because he is subconsciously telling you something that is important to him.

Watch particularly for any *sudden or dramatic* increase or decrease in movement, and *abrupt* changes in verbal and vocal styles. For example, if the person you're talking to suddenly moves his torso dramatically: twists or turns away, bends down or throws his shoulders back, or even unexpectedly gets up and walks away, pay close attention. Again, his subconscious is leaking a message you should be reading.

If a person suddenly and repeatedly crosses and uncrosses his legs, he is trying to relieve stress and is definitely expressing himself in one of the moods.

Alert yourself if the person abruptly stops speaking, or his voice suddenly gets softer or louder or higher in pitch; if he starts speaking very quickly or obviously slows down; and especially if he suddenly starts saying things in a way he doesn't normally express himself.

These are all gross signals of Mood Language that are hard to miss.

However, although it is essential to read these obvious signals, there are hundreds of less obvious signals given off by a person's body and voice that you will become more adept at picking up the more closely you observe. These are the *fleeting signals* that last for less than a second: a quick glance, a momentary grimace, a flick of the hand, or an almost imperceptible change of body position; a brief pause, a quick cough, a minute change of pitch, or even the misuse of a pronoun.

Unless a person is in the habit of using such a movement or vocal or verbal mannerism (for example, a grimace could be a facial tic caused by a neurological condition, or a pause is because of asthma), or there is an obvious cause for it (a flick of the hand could simply be to brush away a fly, or a change of pitch to pronounce a foreign word), there is *some* reason for it and you should attach mood significance to it.

Be aware of as many of these brief signals as possible.

### 2. Clusters
Clusters are groups of three or more signals that send *the same message*, at almost the same time.

For example, if when you're talking to your wife, she suddenly drops her head and shoulders, turns away from you, presses her open hands over her eyes, and starts sobbing, you can be pretty sure you are reading a cluster of signals which *all* tell you, unmistakably, that she is deeply depressed.

Similarly, if she suddenly throws back her head and shoulders, turns away from you, presses her clenched fists to her temples, and lets out a growl of exasperation, you can be certain you are reading a cluster of signals which *all* express that she is definitely very angry—and angry *at you.*

Her abrupt head and shoulder movements and her turning away from you signal rejection. The signals that follow this rejection signal are in keeping with and corroborate the rejection. They cluster.

While these two examples use obvious behavior signals to illustrate the point, the importance of reading clusters rather than individual signals is vital when a person's behavior is more subtle.

For instance if, while you are talking to your wife about something important, she keeps nodding and has a smile on her face, you might assume by reading these two individual signals that she is agreeing with you. But you could be wrong.

Two signals are not enough to read anything into. Look for more than two signals that support and substantiate the message you think you are receiving.

If, on observing your wife more closely, you notice that her smile seems slightly stiff and has been on her face a little too long, that she is showing only her upper teeth, and that her eyes are not smiling, you are reading a cluster of four signals that are sending a very different message.

If to that cluster you add the corroborating evidence of her nods being a little too abrupt and a little too frequent, together with the fact that she is sitting stiff and erect, that her arms are in close to her body, and her feet "planted" on the floor, you are getting a message from someone who is in fact extremely angry.

You now have nine signals—each of which supports and substantiates the same message. Together, these form a reliable cluster that you can confidently read as Anger.

Even though, on the surface, your wife may want you to think she agrees with what you're saying, by reading the signals she is sending out *in complete clusters,* the truth cannot fail to escape you.

### 3. Voice and body signals work in tandem

What people do and the way they do it are usually "echoed" in what they say and the way they say it.

For example, when people are happy, their bodies "act" happy, and their voices "sound" happy; if they're sad, their bodies droop, their faces look downcast, their voices drop and slow, and they express what they want to say in sad and depressing terms.

The clusters of signals you get from a person's verbal behavior should *synchronize* and cluster neatly with the signals you get from his/her non-verbal behavior.

If, however, you receive signals from a person's physical behavior that tell you one thing and signals from the verbal behavior that tell you something different—and there is no neat, synchronized cluster that can be read clearly—an alarm should sound in your mind. That person is trying to hide something from you.

Since most people think that others rely merely on what they *say,* they use speech alone to tell others what they want them to believe. They forget that their bodies are saying something else. They are trying to hide their real meaning from other people.

So, when the messages from a person's voice and from his or her body are "out of sync" with each other, place more reliance on what his or her body language is telling you.

## 4. Proxemics

Dr. Edward T. Hall's theory states that there are certain distances or "zones of territory" a person keeps between him- or herself and another person in order to create a tacit understanding between them.

These zones are:

> Intimate distance 6 ins–18 ins
> Personal distance 18 ins–4 ft
> Social distance    4 ft–12 ft
> Public distance    12 ft–25+ ft

As the names of these divisions suggest, a person uses each of these zones to communicate intimate, personal, social, or public messages, respectively.

When it comes to reading a person's Mood Language, it is important to observe which of these distances he/she uses in each of the moods.

For instance, a person in the Mood of Depression who moves in very close to you is trying to manipulate you into bonding with him—he is trying to tell you that he really wants to be comforted.

However, if he moves as far away from you as he can, he is expressing that he wants to be left alone with his Depression and definitely does not want to bond. He is really telling you to go away.

If, in the Mood of Bargaining, someone who normally stays four to twelve feet from you (your social zone) suddenly moves in very close to you—into your intimate zone—you can be sure she is trying to cajole you into giving her something.

The way a person changes the space between him- or herself and you is a useful Mood Language signal that should be read in a complete cluster with other synchronized signals.

### 5. Fight-or-flight reaction

W. B. Cannon coined this expression in 1929 to describe how a person reacts when threatened. The reaction is inherited from the time when primitive man, startled by the sudden appearance of a predator or an unexpected movement, had to decide on the spur of the moment either to stand and fight or flee for his life. At this moment the heart beats faster, the liver releases glucose into the bloodstream, and the adrenaline starts pumping.

In Mood Language, where it is primarily another person's rejection that is threatening, a person's initial surprise or shock at being rejected sets off a mental, emotional, and physical reaction that causes them to look quickly away or blink, momentarily breaking eye contact.

They use this moment to rapidly take stock of the situation and evaluate their position. During this brief evaluation period, they are caught up in the fight-or-flight syndrome as they try to decide whether to attack or to cut and run.

Having decided (for rational and/or emotional reasons) to either fight or flee, they determine which one of the four Moods of Rejection offers the greatest leverage over their opponent. They then consciously and subconsciously slip into the language of that chosen mood.

### 6. A person's body is extremely expressive

It is impossible for a person consciously to control every alteration of the heart rate, every variation of respiratory activity, every change in muscle responses, and every movement of his or her body.

People cannot help but express themselves through their bodies. And all their bodily "expressions" are there to be seen and read by anyone who cares to watch for them.

Train yourself to be observant: look and *see* every movement, however small, the person you are reading makes.

While a person's whole body is expressive, the *face* is the easiest part of the body to read because the muscles of the face, which react rapidly to any type of stress, are exposed to full view.

Since we subconsciously focus on each other's faces when we're communicating anyway, it is not difficult to train your eye to register and read even the most minute movement in this largest exposed group of muscles.

Always keep in mind the "normal" look of a person's face, then watch for all movements of eyebrows, forehead, lips, tongue, and for any facial tics or spasms that may suddenly change that normal look.

Also note particularly any touching of the face, especially in the areas of the mouth and nose.

Be aware of slight changes in skin tone (reddening or paling), which indicate certain mood shifts.

The *eyes*, particularly, betray emotions. It is very difficult for anyone to prevent his or her true feelings from showing in the eyes, and as up to 60 percent of our communication is usually carried on through eye contact, you should train yourself to pick up any and every change of expression in a person's eyes.

## SIGNIFICANT MOOD LANGUAGE EXPRESSIONS

The following sections are intended to give you an overall, general picture of *what* someone in each of the moods does and says, and *why* he/she says and does it in the way he/she does. In reading their Mood Language, you should be able to recognize and understand the exact meaning of their behavior.

A checklist of the main features and most important expressions of the language of each of the moods is contained in the Appendix. Read quickly through the Appendix after you have finished this chapter, and turn to it for reference as your "reading" skill improves.

Anger

A person who is angry is trying to fight rejection, and she uses whatever is at her disposal to attack not only the person who has made her angry, but anything and everything that gets in her way.

Because she is fighting so hard, her body is in a state of high arousal: all her muscles are tight and flexing for combat.

Her face muscles are taut, and when she is not talking, her lips are either clamped together or drawn back. You may even see a muscle throbbing at her temple or neck.

If you see a muscle tic at the side of one or both eyes, you should know she is trying very hard to hold her anger in check. If she starts biting her lips or tongue, she is trying to control what she wants to blurt out.

Her eyes are hard and cold, and she doesn't blink as frequently as she does normally. She might even try to "stare down" her opponent in an effort to dominate him.

She also needs to relieve her stress and frustration at being rejected by venting her anger as quickly and dramatically as possible, so she uses this dramatic "venting" to dominate, control, and manipulate the other person who has rejected her, and, in a spirit of revenge, to stress and upset him in return.

In attacking the other person, she launches into an assault on everything she can think of: who he is, what he stands for, the way he thinks, the way he feels, his values, his position. The angrier she gets, the greater her scale and range of attack becomes.

She also latches onto trivial, irrelevant details and vents her ire on those. In fact, she will assail anything that allows her to deflect responsibility away from herself and blame anyone or anything else.

We all know the gross physical signals a person sends out when he's angry: his movements are jerky, his chin juts out, his hands may clench and unclench, and he breathes more

loudly than he normally does. If his hands are not gesticulating dramatically, pounding or pointing, his arms are drawn
in close to his body or crossed over his chest.

But there are a number of other signals that are not usually
known to be signs of anger. These are usually signals of
anger being kept *under control,* and you should be aware of
some of them at this stage.

You are reading *latent* anger if you see:

- A smile freeze on a person's face as his eyes start to
  stare coldly at you.
- One or both of his shoulders begin to rise.
- The arms he has crossed over his chest start rising
  higher and higher as he gets angrier and angrier.
- His hands form a "figure L," with his thumb below
  his chin and his index finger extended up the side of
  his face.
- One hand begins to rub at the back of his neck—this
  may signal a prelude to physical violence.

> Anger directed at something inanimate has a calming effect and
> brings relief quicker than when it is aimed at a person.

### Depression

A person who is depressed is trying to flee from what he
thinks is not only your rejection of him but also the world's.

He is hurting. He can't take any more and tries to ward off
any further attack on him from outside. So he turns his anger
in on himself and attacks himself to save others the trouble.

Because he has "given up," his body slows down and he
becomes lethargic. His speech becomes softer and slower,
and he often will not even bother to complete his sentences,
letting his thoughts just trail off.

He is so locked in on his own pain that he can't concentrate on what is happening around him, and he frequently misunderstands or completely misses a great deal of what you're saying to him.

At the same time, he tries to comfort and soothe himself, and to justify his not being able to do anything to correct the situation that's depressing him.

He tries to get you to understand his position and sympathize with him. So he talks about how difficult "life" is for him: he tells you in great detail how much whatever it is that's depressed him is costing him and how deeply he is affected by it. If it sways you, he will also tell you about how he's not sleeping or eating properly and how his health is being affected.

In trying to manipulate you into bonding with him, he attacks himself for all his failings, and will probably even tell you you are better off without him. He wants you to protest and prove him wrong.

We all know what people look like when they are depressed; but again, there are certain signals and their meanings, which are not generally understood. Some that you should be aware of are:

- When a person in Depression starts breathing (or even crying) in an audible, exaggerated way, he is trying to communicate to you that he wants your attention.
- In Depression, a person touches his face more frequently than normal. He may rub at or cover his eyes, pull at or cover his mouth, rub the sides of his face or head, and hold his head in his hands.
- A person who strokes at the inside of his thighs is trying to soothe his depression and comfort himself.
- If a person subconsciously forms a "suicide finger" with his index finger extended and pointed at his temple, his thumb pointing upward and his palm curled

backward, he is in very deep Depression and needs
your help.

> Depression is the most painful Mood of Rejection, and Anger is
> always just below the surface.

### Bargaining

A person in the Mood of Bargaining is trying to both fight
against, and flee from, rejection.

Her bargaining behavior is usually overly solicitous and too
"nice." You will see a great number of submission signals as
she tries to show you you have nothing to fear from her. She
moves into a closer "zone of territory" than she normally
uses and touches you more frequently than she usually does.
Her eye contact becomes excessive and she smiles too often
and for too long.

As her motive is to get you to stop rejecting her and bond
with her again, she does anything that will make this happen.
She needs to deactivate any conflict as quickly as she can, so
she may even tell you she's wrong and you're right—even
though she doesn't really believe what she's saying.

She doesn't want you to reject her any further, so if it looks
as if you are going to attack her again, she tries to ward off
your assault by telling you what a good person she really is:
what she's done for you in the past, what you or others have
said about how "thoughtful and considerate" she is, about
what a good "wife/girlfriend/mother/daughter" (or "hus-
band/boyfriend/father/son") she is, and even may try to explain to you how religious she is!

She could try to ward off your attack by telling you how ill
she is: how her blood pressure is too high, or her nervous
condition is acting up, or what her doctor told her on her last
visit. She will demonstrate the appropriate physical behavior
to reinforce this argument.

She'll start using pet names, flatter you outrageously, make all sorts of promises about what she'll never do again or what she will do in the future, and offer inducements like gifts or treats or sexual favors.

She tries to convince you that your needs are of primary importance and hers are only secondary, so she'll take whatever deal you offer, provided you'll just stop rejecting her.

Signals of bargaining to watch out for particularly are:

- Crying that occurs too quickly and at inappropriate times. This is used to manipulate you into feeling sorry for her.
- Glancing toward the ceiling, which implies "You've got to believe me—I'm helpless in this situation."
- Holding her hands out toward you, palm upward. This is an obvious submission signal.
- Tones of voice that are cajoling, wheedling, conciliatory, and altogether too "sincere" to ring true.
- Excessive flattery and/or flirtation.

> Bargaining is the mood closest to Acceptance and shows the least number of obvious rejection signals.

### Denial

A person who is in Denial is attempting to flee rejection. He does this in one of two ways: either by denying the truth to himself through self-deception; or by denying the truth to others through lying.

The Mood Language of the cheating husband who was confronted by his wife, which was described in Chapter 4, is a typical example of the second form of Denial.

However, it is the language of the first form—Denial through self-deception—that is most important in reading Mood Language.

A person who is in this form of Denial cannot face the reality of being rejected and attempts to convince himself that nothing is "wrong." He wants simply to dismiss the thought of whatever it is that would upset him so badly if he faced it. He does not want to acknowledge it, discuss it, or even admit it exists, so he tries to act as normally as possible. Apart from his behavior appearing to be a little forced and strained, and the fact that from time to time you might catch him looking at you with a worried expression, there is very little you can read in what he says and does.

If, however, you bring up the issue he is so determined to ignore, you force him to face the very thing he does not want to deal with, and his Denial behavior becomes very obvious.

He stammers and stutters, he "hems" and "haws," he shuffles his feet and begins to adjust his clothing or pick imaginary lint off the furniture. He looks at his watch or even suddenly decides it is a good time to clean his glasses. These are all stalling tactics designed to "buy time" or throw you off the subject.

Should these preliminary ploys fail to distract you from the subject, he will probably ask you to repeat what you just said, or he may even repeat it out loud himself with a look of disbelief on his face.

Should you persist in questioning him, he will not answer you directly but will tell you a great deal about all sorts of other things—which usually have little to do with the main issue he is denying.

You should notice also that this explanation about anything *but* the main issue becomes more and more emotional.

He may begin talking about other people—and even you—in totally negative and disparaging terms in order to bolster his own threatened self-image.

Some of the less obvious signals of Denial you should be aware of are:

- An increase in normal blink rate.
- A hand hovering around the mouth more than normal and actually covering the mouth as a sentence is disrupted before its completion.
- Thumb and index finger playing with the lower part of the nose as the person in Denial says or is about to say something he does not really believe himself.
- One hand thrown away from the body to dismiss an idea or question.
- Frequent use of expressions like "I can't remember," "Not that I can think of," or "I don't *think* so."
- Incomplete sentences, restarted sentences, and sentences picked up in the middle—when he knows you are not being taken in by his Denial.
- Sudden use of third-person words—"others," "they," "them," "everybody," "no one"—as an appeal to universal acknowledgment of his own version of reality.

---

The language of Denial has the greatest range of all the Moods of Rejection and is the mood most often used.

---

### "Submission" Signals

In the world of high-stress criminal interviewing, there are a number of signals that indicate a guilty suspect has reached the point of no return, abrogated all his (or her) will and power to the interviewer, and is about to make a full and detailed confession.

Some of these signs are:

1. Holding and/or rubbing the chin while smiling
2. Rubbing the upper and lower lips together for 15–30 seconds
3. Eyes rolling back into the head followed by closing of the eyelids
4. Eyes raised to the ceiling accompanied by very slow blink rate
5. The open palms of the hands suddenly turning upward
6. A deep sigh followed by a dropping of the shoulders and the chin sinking to the chest

7. A sudden, inexplicable "leaning forward" into the interviewer's body space as if to get close
8. The sudden raising of both hands in an almost military
   "surrender" gesture
9. The entire upper body suddenly relaxing and "blos-
   soming open" as if to make the heart and chest area vulnerable as a "target."

However, be warned that the world of mutually caring and loving relationships is very different from the world of the police interviewer and the criminal. If in the course of an argument you
see any of these signals being sent out, you should stop whatever it is you are saying or doing immediately.

You may have won your argument in the short run, but in the
long run, after the moment of domination and victory is over, all
you will have done is foster a deep and lasting resentment of
your power that may be very difficult (if not impossible) ever to
rectify.

---

## Just Say No

If people say no and mean no they will say it directly, shortly,
and unequivocally because it is the truth.

But if when they say no, what they really mean is yes, they
will frequently give themselves away by the way they say that
no.

If, in answer to a direct question, they say no not as they normally say it, but in one of the following ways, you can be sure
they are lying to you:

1. "N-o-o-o . . ." (a long-drawn-out no).
2. ". . . No." (a long pause before no).
3. "No, no, no, no!" (repeated several times).
4. A no preceded or followed by a nervous laugh, chuck-
   ling, or inappropriate amusement.
5. A no while nodding the head to mean yes.
6. A no followed by closing the eyes or putting one hand
   over the mouth.
7. A no accompanied by an exaggerated shaking of the entire body.
8. A no followed by a quick glance away.
9. A no followed by a sudden crossing of the arms and/or
   legs.
10. A no answer to your question *before you have even fin-
    ished asking it.*

# SEVEN

# How to Respond to Moods

## UNDERSTANDING AND SATISFYING ANOTHER'S NEEDS

The goal of the *3Rs* is Mutual Acceptance. We want to lead each other through our mutual rejection into Acceptance. We want to love each other again.

We don't just want to stop the fighting, the arguing, the bickering, the snide remarks, or even just the feeling of loneliness and separateness; we genuinely want to understand and satisfy the deepest needs of this person, and love them— and we want them to love us in the same way.

The power to do this lies in knowing how to respond to the moods of the person we love.

We want to respond to who they really are and to what they're really telling us, so that we can understand and meet those needs they are so desperately but ineptly trying to communicate with their Mood Language.

Once we know and can read why and how they are using Denial, Anger, Depression, and Bargaining to get us to understand them, we have the master key to direct access to their needs.

How we deal with and satisfy those needs depends on how we respond to their varying Moods of Denial, Anger, Depression, and Bargaining.


## THE POWER OF RESPONSE

Moods do not exist in a vacuum. They are activated by stress. Even when we are alone, our moods intensify, weaken, or shift because of what we believe others are doing or not doing to us—or even what we believe others are thinking or not thinking about us. Other people probably have more control over our moods than we do ourselves. Their attitudes and responses can either intensify or weaken our moods.

This is especially true when the "other person" is someone whose very acceptance and approval gives us a sense of well-being about who we are, and whose rejection has the exact opposite effect on us. It is as if this person has the power of control over our moods. He or she has the power to propel us up and down, in and out of such moods.

They exercise this control over us by the way they respond to us. For example, imagine that you've just had some wonderful news. You are delighted by it, and you feel so elated you want to tell someone about it. You call your lover at work to share your happiness with him, but he's too busy to listen and cuts you short. He dismisses you by saying he'll hear it this evening, then puts the phone down on you.

Your pleasurable mood has evaporated. The way he responded to you has shifted you out of Acceptance and hurled you into the Moods of Rejection. You can't even think of your good news in the same way anymore. You begin to resent him for doing this to you and you are irked at the power of control he seems to have over you. Your whole afternoon is now seen through the viewpoint of rejection. You will fester until you can let him know exactly what you think of him this evening.

Just as his response to you has altered your mood for the worse—and just as your intended response to him this evening will certainly alter his—each of us also has the power to alter another person's mood for the better. It all depends on *how we respond* to that other person's moods.

We have the power to shepherd each other from the depths of rejection to the heights of Acceptance. And that is our goal.

## STEPS TO ACHIEVE THE GOAL OF ACCEPTANCE

There are three steps to get the person we care for (or anyone else) to accept us.
We must:

1. Neutralize our own moods.
2. Read the other person's Mood Language.
3. Respond in order to meet the needs of each mood.

### 1. Neutralizing Our Own Moods

Rejection is a mutual affair. As we have seen, if we are dealing with someone who is rejecting us, we have a natural tendency to slip into one or other of the Moods of Rejection ourselves.

However, if we are in any of the Moods of Rejection ourselves, we cannot possibly address other people's needs wholeheartedly. Our own mood interferes with the clear reception of what they are trying to tell us and pits our needs against theirs. So we have to neutralize our own moods and concentrate on theirs. They are to be the whole focus of our attention.

This means that we must not allow ourselves to display any emotional, mental, or physical hint of rejection, no matter how minor or fleeting. We are genuinely trying to understand not only what other people are trying to tell us but *exactly what they mean*—even if they are not aware of it themselves.

It is not enough that we know that is what we're doing; they must be made aware of our intention also. They must be made to feel they are the focus of our full and undivided attention, which is concerned, caring, non-judgmental, and above all neither critical nor rejecting. They must sense our *empathy*.

While we do not have to agree with them, we do have to acknowledge their right to think and feel as they do; and we do have to acknowledge and give value to their sense of justification (in their terms) that they have a right to think and feel the way they do. We must let them know that to us they have worth, value, and dignity in who and what they are—even if we do not see eye to eye on every issue.

It is not easy to remain neutral. We shall be attacked overtly and covertly, we shall have to fight the contagion of their moods, our patience will be sorely tried, and our own needs will be made to seem irrelevant.

And while all this is happening, we must be constantly aware of our own almost automatic tendency to "fight or flee" the person who is rejecting us—and control it.

Difficult as this may sound, remember that we have a secret weapon: we understand what is happening to the other person in these moods, and we have this book to guide us through the steps toward Mutual Acceptance.

Remember also, we are in this position because we want to be: we desperately want this other person's understanding, but we cannot expect to have it until we have given him or her ours.

We must demonstrate that we really care for who and what they are, what they think and feel, before we can expect the *Reciprocation* we long for.

---

### Rules for Neutralizing Moods

*Stay in Acceptance*
— Do not allow yourself to be drawn into their mood
— Do not be judgmental, and never blame: control your body
   language especially
— Do not look for hidden meanings that are not there; read
   complete clusters
— React to show you are listening and trying to understand

*Be genuine—and mean it!*
— Do not feign mental, emotional, or physical sincerity
— Project understanding, empathy, support, and caring

*Give them your full attention*
— Maintain eye contact, especially when you're listening to
   them
— Watch them carefully and see what they're conveying: their
   non-verbal Mood Language will tell you
— Listen to them carefully and hear what their verbal Mood
   Language is telling you
— Pinpoint their central theme

*Do not allow your personality to take over*
— Do not let who you are intrude, dominate, or control
— Be patient: never interrupt or display restlessness

---

2.  Reading the Other Person's Mood Language

In reading other persons' Mood Language, we have to be
aware that whatever mood they may be in, certain essential
needs remain constant. These needs are, like the caveman's
need for food and shelter and warmth, basic and un-
changeable.

Whether or not they realize it, each mood they slip into
merely repeats and reinforces these same basic needs in a
different manner and with a different emphasis.

These essential needs, no matter which form they are presented in, are the need to:

(1.)  protect themselves and their position, either offen-
       sively or defensively;

(2.)  control the direction and flow of the conflict;

(3.)   feel their own emotions and think their own
       thoughts;
(4.)   express their theme;
(5.)   vent their thoughts and feelings, and relieve stress;
(6.)   project their personality; and
(7.)   force you to bond with them by manipulating you
       into accepting their position and, in the case of inti-
       mate relationships, them personally.

## 3.   Responding to the Other Person's Moods

If we are going to lead people out of the mood of Rejection
they're in and guide them through to Acceptance, we have to
respond to these basic needs they are expressing in whatever
form they choose to express them.

They will not move into Acceptance until these needs have
been not only acknowledged but addressed and met to their
satisfaction. Until this happens, they will either stay in one
rejection mood while they stubbornly try to force you to understand their needs, or shift from one mood to another (Bargaining or Anger, Depression or Denial), depending on which
they think will have the most persuasive impact on you.

If you fail to respond to and placate these needs, the person
will be unable to move toward Acceptance and will continue
to fester through these various Moods of Rejection until all
communication breaks down completely.

In other words, unless we can address the deepest needs of
those closest to us, we may find ourselves with no one close
enough to address anything to anyway.

## THINGS YOU MUST AND MUST NOT DO IN RESPONDING TO THEIR NEEDS

### 1. You must allow them to protect themselves and their position

Do not attack them. Do not even challenge them head-on.
Make them aware that you do not intend to assault, assail, or

even argue with them, and that there is absolutely no hostility
in your attitude toward them.

Remember you have neutralized your own moods, and you
are only there to try to understand what they are attempting
to tell you.

Once they realize you are not threatening them in any way,
the energy they have been using to protect themselves in the
more aggressive Moods of Rejection (Denial and Anger) can
be directed somewhere more productive.

### 2. You must persuade them that they do not need to maintain such zealous control over the direction and flow of the conflict.

Initially, they use the different controlling styles of Anger
(domination), Depression (withdrawal into self-flagellation),
Bargaining (teasing you with partial acceptance), and Denial
(blank refusal to face the problem) as a shield against your
rejection of them and their position. They sense that as long
as they are in control, they can prevent any further attacks
from penetrating their defenses.

You must convince them you are not attacking them and
allow them to lower their defenses. Let them know you are
not trying to belittle or devalue their thoughts and feelings—
you are merely trying to understand their position and their
reasons for it.

But do not allow yourself to be manipulated. Be aware of
what they are trying to do and how they are doing it, but do
not become controlled by them. You must—gradually, subtly,
and unaggressively—gain control of the flow of their moods
and usher them toward Acceptance.

### 3. You must give them time to go through and "savor" their thoughts and feelings

Do not rush them through the particular emotions they are
experiencing or the line of thought they are following in each

of the moods. Do not dismiss or denigrate what they are going through. If you disrupt their flow of thought and feeling,
they will remain unsatisfied and keep harking back to that
area and that mood until it has been "experienced" fully. And
you will be made to pay for the disruption.

Leave them alone at those times (especially in Depression
and Anger) when they are not interested in bonding with you
or sharing their needs with you; they simply want to be alone
with their thoughts and feelings. They need to come to terms
with and handle their stress in their own way.

Be patient, watch, and listen sympathetically to what
they're telling you.

### 4. You must encourage them to make their thoughts
### and feelings known

Let them vent. Allow them to purge themselves fully of all
the thoughts and emotions that are causing them distress.
These thoughts and emotions will be expressed both verbally
and non-verbally with vehemence (in Anger), with sorrow (in
Depression), through dismissal (in Denial), and through ne-
gotiation and "horse trading" (in Bargaining).

Hear them out. Let them get everything, real or imagined,
that's upsetting them off their chest. Do not react negatively
to anything you see or hear, even when it is aimed at you
personally; simply follow the flow attentively. Look on it as a
"cleansing process" that is getting rid of their pain and healing their wounds.

### 5. You must pick up on and isolate their theme

The real reason for their conflict is in their *theme,* which is
being repeated directly and indirectly in different ways in
each of the Moods of Rejection. At times it will be expressed
precisely, whereas at other times it will be merely hinted at.
It is delivered blatantly or subtly in the accusations of blame
in Anger, in the self-cutting reproaches of Depression, in the

negative assertions of Denial, and in the circuitous demands of Bargaining.

But it is the *repetition*—in whatever guise—of the single line of underlying motive that allows you to isolate their central theme.

Paraphrase what you think their theme is and repeat it back to them. If you are right, they will verify it. If you are wrong, they will just keep repeating it in various ways through the moods until you do get it right.

Once you have isolated their theme, address it directly. You must acknowledge it, give it importance and value, and show that you are trying to understand it. Relate all the apparently extraneous issues that have been brought up back to this central theme.

While most times they will want to discuss their theme in depth, there are other times when they will not invite you to respond in any way other than to show you understand it. (See [3] above.)

### 6. You must allow them to give "full rein" to their personality

The natural way each of the personality types uses and abuses Mood Language must be tolerated and accepted. Do not try to make them act or talk the way *you* want them to; let them assert who they are in their own way. Under stress, their core personality is being drawn on, and this *cannot* be altered.

On no account must you allow your irritation, impatience, or pain over the way they are doing and saying things to show. Your rejection of their personality style will only force them to become more and more entrenched in their Moods of Rejection.

**7. You must convince them your bond with them has not been broken, even though you do not agree with them on this particular issue**

Show them that it is *because* your mutual approval is so important to you that you are trying so hard to understand their contrary point of view in this instance.

Let them know you are not rejecting who and what they are—that in fact you *love* them the way they are. It is because you love them that you are trying to see and understand their position.

The following charts shows what a person in each of the Moods of Rejection needs to do and how you should respond to that need.

THE MOODS OF REJECTION:
WHAT A PERSON IN *ANGER* NEEDS TO DO
AND HOW YOU SHOULD RESPOND

**THEY NEED TO:**

1. *Vent their Anger.*
   All their seething, bottled-up thoughts and emotions need to be stated out loud in a direct, dramatic, and forceful manner. They need to "experience" the passion of all their negative emotions and relieve their stress.

   They do *not* need to stay controlled and unexpressive, nor do they want to express their views in a calm, rational manner.

2. *Dominate, control, and manipulate you and the situation.*
   They need to believe they have complete and total

**YOU MUST:**

1. *Stay in neutral.*
   Show that you are listening and trying to understand. Any "opinion" that is being vented cannot be changed in Anger. Simply allow their Anger to run its full course and burn itself out.

   You must *not* allow yourself to get pulled into responsive Anger; shift into any other mood; interrupt or voice an opinion; or suggest they "Calm down."

2. *Allow them to believe they have total control.*
   Until their Anger has been fully vented and abates of its own accord

power of command. They
want to either (i) pressure
you into agreeing with
them and forcing a bond, or
(ii) drive you away from
them to prove they do not
want to bond.

They do *not* want to be si-
lenced, squashed, inter-
rupted, challenged, or
crossed in any way.

3. *Force the issue.*
They want to bring every-
thing to a head, out in the
open. They need to lay
blame and justify them-
selves and their stance.
They want to declaim their
theme in the most em-
phatic way possible.

They do *not* want to be
told they're wrong.

4. *Create friction.*
They will look for any excuse to attack you in order
to justify and strengthen
their Anger and will pro-
voke and bait you to get a
reaction. They will pounce
on any pretext (real or
imagined) to sustain their
irritation.

They do *not* want you be
to totally non-responsive—
this does not suit their purposes.

you can do nothing. Allow
them to dominate and con-
trol but do *not* allow them
to manipulate you. Answer
their direct questions as
succinctly and factually as
possible (without emotional
nuances or pushing your
difference of opinion).

You must *not* challenge,
interrupt, squash or silence
them or attempt to take
control.

3. *Let them air all their negative thoughts and feelings.*
Listen to what they're
claiming the problem is
and whose fault they think
it is. Whether or not they're
exaggerating the truth, this
is what they believe in this
Mood. Take it seriously.
Pick up on their theme but
do not address it until their
mood has cooled.

You must *not* show any
sign of disagreement or impatience.

4. *Accept that their Anger is
looking for anything and everything to attack.*
If challenged to voice
your disagreement, stay in
neutral and simply respond
that you can see why they
must think/feel the way
they do.

You must *not* give them
any opportunity to create
more friction and make
their Anger last longer than
it needs to.

5.  *Be impervious to you.*
    They need to close themselves off from being favorably affected by your thoughts and feelings. Your point of view is irrelevant.

    They do *not* need to be aware that you have a different viewpoint.

5.  *Accept that they are imperious to your needs at this stage.*
    If they are not trying to bond with you and your mere presence is exacerbating their Anger, get away. If you are merely being used as a soundingboard, listen sympathetically.

    You must *not* fuel their Anger by making your contrary opinions and feelings obvious.

### THE MOODS OF REJECTION: WHAT A PERSON IN *DEPRESSION* NEEDS TO DO AND HOW YOU SHOULD RESPOND

THEY NEED TO:

1.  *"Experience" their pain.*
    The full gamut of self-attacking and self-destructive thoughts and emotions has to be played through and allowed to hurt. Sometimes they need to experience it alone *initially*, in private, until they can share their misery.

    They do *not* want their pain to be dismissed, undervalued, or ignored.

YOU MUST:

1.  *React sympathetically.*
    Try to understand what they are going through but do not intrude on their pain. Respond only after they have expressed their distress. Listen if they want to talk and follow the flow, paying close attention to the theme of their Depression. Interruption is viewed as Rejection. Be patient. If they want to be alone, let them.

    You must *not:* shift into any Rejection Mood; voice your own opinion on why they are depressed; suggest they "pull themselves together" or "snap out of it."

2.  *Be the focus of attention and concern.*
    Their pain needs to be the only thing both you and they are interested in. They

2.  *Forget anything else you may have on your mind.*
    You are there to reflect back their pain to show it is being bonded with.

need you to feel and understand the depth and intensity of their distress.

They do *not* need you to see their Depression objectively—they need an empathetic, subject view of it.

3. *Express their pain.*
   When they are ready, they need to communicate how they think and feel, and either state directly or hint at the reasons for their Depression.

They do *not* want you to assume you know the reasons for their Depression.

4. *Have their pain understood.*
   They need to explore their discomfort and the reasons (real or imagined) for it with someone who can sympathize with them. They want it addressed and understood in *their* terms, i.e., emotional or logical. They feel helpless, lost, lonely, and alone—they are

You must *not* dominate them or the situation, take control with your personality, or try to influence the flow.

3. *Be aware of when they are ready to talk about their Depression.*
   Listen carefully and sympathetically, only talking to utter brief expressions of understanding. Let them vent completely. Do not talk unless they make it obvious a response is required. Keep your reply brief or ask a question of them to direct attention back to them.
   When they say why they feel this way, accept their reasoning at face value. Do not disagree or take it as a personal attack. Pick up on their theme but do not address it yet.

You must *not* allow your disagreement with their reasoning to drive you into a Rejection Mood.

4. *Focus on their theme.*
   Articulate it for verification. Address it in the same terms they have used: emotional or logical. Let them know you understand why they feel and think the way they do but that theirs is not the *only* way to see the problem. Start discussing their theme objectively. Ex-

trying to bond with you by sharing their pain with you.

They do *not* want their pain to remain unshared.

5. *Be released from their Depression.*
Unless and until they can see a way out of Depression they know the pain will continue, so they search for any valid escape from it. They often suggest solutions in terms of "if only. . . ." They are hoping you will be able to show them the way out.

They do *not* want you to leave them floundering in this state.

plore all the ramifications of the problem. Make them realize they do not have to face the problem alone.

You must *not* allow your own, subjective view to color your approach.

5. *Discuss solutions.*
An in-depth discussion of their theme will have revealed a number of ways the problem can be handled. Encourage them to settle on one of the ways and plan how to implement it. If they are still unable to made a decision, choose a way for them, and then plan together how to carry it out. Let them know your *combined* strength and resolve will solve the problem.

You must *not* suggest unworkable or fake solutions.

## THE MOODS OF REJECTION: WHAT A PERSON IN *BARGAINING* NEEDS TO DO AND HOW YOU SHOULD RESPOND

**THEY NEED TO:**

1. *Protect themselves from attack.*
Any perceived threat to them has to be deflected. Direct, frontal attacks especially need to be prevented at any cost.

**YOU MUST:**

1. *Be aware that Bargaining is the closest mood to Acceptance.*
Any direct, frontal attack will regress the mood, but your displays of discontent, hurt, and mild annoyance will sustain the bonding attempts of Bargaining till you can reach Acceptance.

You must *not* allow Bargaining to shift into a deeper Mood of Rejection.

2. *Shield their own Denial and minimize their faults.*
They need to feel their position is justified in the circumstances, that there are valid reasons for their stance and therefore they are not being unreasonable.

2. *Avoid challenging them directly.*
Acknowledge that you can understand why and how they think and feel the way they do, and that from their point of view their actions were justified *but* . . . : then give your perspective and your reasons patiently and logically, without laying blame, while displaying how you have lost out and been hurt.

They do *not* want to admit or acknowledge openly that they are *solely* at fault.

You must *not* confront their Denial directly or overemphasize their faults. Do not force them to admit, out loud, total responsibility for fault.

3. *Adopt a peripheral approach.*
Because of their dislike of frontal attack they need to tackle the problem obliquely—concentrating on minor aspects of the problem to prove their point of view is correct and justified

3. *Patiently allow them to approach the problem in their own roundabout way.*
Meet each point they make sympathetically but conclude every point by logically relating it back to the central issue. Read their many-stranded theme carefully and try to identify its core concern.

You must *not* try to dominate or take control of the approach by dismissing any peripheral issues as unimportant or irrelevant

4. *Be seen as fair, evenhanded, and considerate.*
They need you to acknowledge that there is no malice behind their actions

4. *Allow them to see you are not being satisfied.*
Tell them you know their motives are not perverse and that you realize they

and that *your* interests are *also* being taken into account. They need to feel they are establishing empathy and bonding with you.

are considering your needs as well *but* that your real needs are in fact being frustrated. Explain this dilemma (without suggesting any of this is their fault) and ask for their suggestions on how you should handle it and them. Their theme will be easier to pinpoint in their reply. Take advantage of their concessions and build on them.

They do *not* want to believe they are thinking *only* of themselves and satisfying only themselves.

You must *not* confront them aggressively with your dissatisfaction but adopt a "soft," kind, and non-controling approach.

5. *Feel there is a spirit of give-and-take.*
   They will offer to give something but need to feel they are getting something in return. They believe they deserve to be rewarded for giving first.

5. *Make it obvious that you are giving them your understanding.*
   Address their theme and show you understand what they want and why they want it. Then place it in an objective—not merely your own—context and discuss the give-and-take on both sides. Emphasize what you are giving up to meet their needs.

They do *not* need to feel they are doing all the giving.

You must *not* allow them to feel that they are being more generous than you are.

6. *Get the best deal they can.*
   They need to believe that, in the circumstances, there is *mutual* satisfaction, and that what they have received is only just and fair.

6. *Make sure they are satisfied.*
   Then make them feel you are pleased with the compromise that has been worked out and that you appreciate what they have given up to satisfy your needs.

They do *not* want you to believe you have been left with the short end of the stick unjustly and could therefore continue to reject them.

You must *not* leave them with the feeling they have somehow lost out.

### THE MOODS OF REJECTION:
### WHAT A PERSON IN *DENIAL* NEEDS TO DO
### AND HOW YOU SHOULD RESPOND
### (This is Denial in Form 1: Denial of the truth to self or self-deception)

**THEY NEED TO:**

1. *Hide in Denial.*
   They need to put up a barrier against the truth. They are not capable of facing the reality of a situation or even *trying* to come to terms with it yet. They need to protect themselves from the harmful effects of the truth by convincing themselves nothing has happened.

   They do *not* want to be able to see the situation clearly or objectively.

2. *Avoid facing the truth.*
   They need to cling to anything that prevents them from having to acknowledge the truth: by totally ignoring it, by convincing themselves it does not alter anything, by believing they are the only ones interpreting the facts correctly.

**YOU MUST:**

1. *Stay in Neutral.*
   Allow them to absorb the shock in their own time and try to come to terms with the truth without your interference. Most Denial is temporary, and they may be able to come out of it themselves.

   You must *not* immediately force them to confront the truth directly—this will send them deeper into Denial.

2. *Make them aware that you know the truth.*
   No matter what they may want to believe themselves, or want you to believe, every time they do or say something that ignores the truth, tell them logically, calmly, and non-judgmentally why *you* can't go along with their reasoning. Tell them matter-of-factly.

   Pick up their theme and try to identify what their core fear of accepting the truth really is.

They do *not* want to be shown they are wrong.

You must *not* respond emotionally even if they react in Anger, or try to force them to agree with your point of view.

3. *Convince themselves they are not deceiving themselves.*
Any argument—however illogical—will be used to prove to themselves they are right. They fear they will diminish themselves in their own eyes and not be able to face themselves.

3. *Stay out of their internal mental wrestling.*
If they try to justify their behavior to you, do not react negatively. Listen with interest and show that you are trying sympathetically to understand why they think what they do. Allow them to know you think otherwise without saying so directly. Listen carefully for their underlying theme.

They do *not* need to be humiliated or belittled.

You must *not* give them the impression you will reject them if they admit to the truth.

4. *Convince you that their point of view is correct.*
Depending on the intensity of their Denial, they will use anything that will work on you: outright lies, trickery, evasion, pretense, stubbornness; Bargaining, Anger, and Depression.

4. *Remain unswayed.*
Let them know that, to you, the truth is so obvious, that whatever they say or do you will not be convinced otherwise. Draw their attention to the evidence and how, to you, it is undeniable. Gently try to point out all the factual and—in the context of an argument—emotional evidence that may help persuade them to accept the reality of the situation.
Be prepared for their sudden shifts into the other Moods of Rejection in their manipulative attempts to win you over.

They do *not* want you to remain convinced otherwise

You must *not* allow them to think that if they persist in their line of reasoning or

manipulation they will ever
succeed in persuading you
to see things their way.

**5.** *Block out the inevitable consequences of facing the
truth.*
      They fear what will hap-
pen if they accept the truth.
They doubt they will be
able to cope with the consequences, especially your rejection of them. They fear
being generally ostracized.

**5.** *Emphasize the advantages
of acceptance of the truth.*
      Stress the beneficial ef-
fects to themselves, yourself, and your relationship.
Make them understand
that, much as you want to,
you cannot really trust
them if they continue to
deny the reality of the situation and that your relationship is being adversely affected.
      Address their main cause
of concern—their theme—
and suggest ways of dealing
with it. Show them that if
they accept the truth, you
will still care for them and
will work the problem
through with them sympa-
thetically. Let them know
they will not have to face
the consequences alone.

      They do *not* want to face
the greater rejection they
think will follow their acknowledgment of the truth.

      You must *not* abandon
them.

## RESPONDING TO RAPIDLY CHANGING MOODS

While the person who is rejecting you may remain in one
mood for some time, he or she may just as likely shift, rapidly
and repeatedly, in and out of all four moods in a very short
space of time.

If this happens, follow the same Steps to Achieve the Goal
of Acceptance (p. 114) and apply the same basic rules on Responding to the Other Person's Moods. (p. 117).

When several moods come at you in rapid succession,

*If you can identify the theme,* you should address that mood which delivers the theme in the most intense way;

*If you cannot identify the theme,* you should try to deal with the moods in the following order:

1. Bargaining (because it contains the least amount of outright rejection)
2. Depression (because it may only require a sympathetic response)
3. Denial (because it is a very difficult mood to sway)
4. Anger (because there is nothing you can do about Anger except allow it to vent)

An example of moods coming thick and fast was seen in Chapter 5 in the exchange between the husband, John, who is being driven crazy over his inability to make Lucy understand that the annual invasion of her family is ruining their own family life, and Lucy, who feels John is responsible for her loneliness.

Once John realized how and why both he and Lucy had been using the Moods of Rejection against each other for so many years, he determined to try for a solution.

In a practice exercise, John rescripted their original exchange. Apart from altering the way he would have brought up the subject in the first place, he rewrote his response to her.

Here is how Lucy had reacted the first time around:

LUCY:

"I love my brother! You're going to have to understand I miss him when he's not here and he misses me.

Locked in *Denial,* she simply ignores his theme and his bonding attempts. She is in total rejection of him and his position.

"Besides, with you on the road so much and the kids away at school all day, I get lonely

Her theme emerges in *Depression:* "You leave me alone and lonely," and in *Bargaining* by

here. Having them all in the house for three weeks is great for me.

"But if you want to change the arrangement, you can talk to him if you like—I don't want to hurt his feelings.

"No. On second thoughts I don't want you to do that. You're so blunt, you'll offend him."

hinting, "So don't I deserve some company?"

She does an about-face out of *Denial* and shifts into *Bargaining,* conceding that he has a point, and offers a deal.

Fearing she will lose out on the deal, she swings back into rejection, using *Denial* of her husband's personality.

Having neutralized his own moods, and read his wife's Mood Language and the theme it contained, John decided he should have responded instead like this:

**JOHN:**

"I know that you're lonely, darling. I probably can't understand how hard it is for you being here by yourself or how difficult it is for you raising the kids virtually by yourself. You've no idea how much it hurts me when I have to leave you alone so often—I'd much rather be home here with you.

"I'll try to cut down the traveling so you won't be so lonely. Maybe you could even come with me some times—we can make arrangements for the kids for a couple of days every month. Or I could look for another job."

Since he can identify her theme emerging in *Depression,* he addresses both the theme and the mood. He responds to it with the rules: being sympathetic, understanding her pain and seeing it in her terms, bonding with it, focusing on her theme, and addressing it.

When he sees that the intensity of her *Depression* is lessening, he proceeds to give her ways out of her *Depression* and the *Denial* within it by discussing joint solutions with her—letting her decide what is best. But his offer to find another job could be dangerous if it is a fake solution, because she could take him up on it and he would then have to reject her.

John then scripted the reply he though Lucy would probably make:

LUCY:

"Well, maybe I could leave the kids for a couple of days.

She comes out of *Depression* into *Acceptance,* bonding with him again, and chooses the suggested solution she feels happiest with.

"Oh, John, I don't how you've carried this 75 hours a week workload you have with that stupid job.

She then shifts into *Bargaining* (shielding her own *Denial* and minimizing her faults) by deflecting blame onto his job.

"Let's see if we can't work out something with my brother. What do you think we could do?

In *Acceptance,* she bonds with him and is willing to discuss jointly made solutions.

"I'll spend more time with you after he goes, or I could . . ."

She slips into *Bargaining* again to get the best deal for herself.

JOHN:

"You suggested that I talk with your brother. I don't want to be blunt or hurt his feelings—I know that would hurt both of you. Between the two of us, what can we come up with to say to him that will make everybody happy in this situation?"

He quickly takes advantage of the concessions she is offering to make in *Bargaining* and picks up on an earlier suggestion of hers. He keeps bonding with her as he plays on her *Bargaining* need to be seen as fair and even-handed.

Confident that he was now able to "manipulate" his wife back into Acceptance, and feeling sure they would work out a solution to the annual invasion, John decided to tackle her face to face.

Knowing Lucy so well, John felt sure he had anticipated everything she would say accurately.

On one level, he had. Yet it was not until they actually began to search for solutions to their problem together, and began loving things about each other again, that he realized for the first time just how much her moods and the way she used them were an integral part of her personality—that it was in fact the way Lucy used the moods that made her personality what it is.

He also realized for the first time—because of the way she used those moods—that the way Lucy saw the world might not necessarily be the same way he saw it, and that things that might mean nothing to him could, in contrast, mean a great deal to her. For the first time in their lives together, John began to be able to tune in to Lucy's wavelength and reach her in a way he had never been able to do before.

We can all do this in our own way with the person most important to us in our own lives, provided we understand that the final step hinges on a realization that what drives each of us to see the world the way we do is what is called the "Dominant Mood" of our individual personality type.

EIGHT

# How to Tune In on a Person's Dominant Mood and Lead Him or Her into Acceptance

### DEFINING THE DOMINANT MOOD

Each personality type has a Dominant Mood, which prescribes the way he or she sees and interprets the world.

Each of the four types' particular view of "their" world is perceived through the lens of one the four Moods of Rejection, which is their Dominant Mood.

The *Feeler* uses the Dominant Mood of Bargaining;
The *Driver* uses the Dominant Mood of Anger;
The *Analyzer* uses the Dominant Mood of Denial;
The *Elitist* uses the Dominant Mood of Depression.

The view through this lens gives each personality type his or her own peculiar and distinct view of "reality," which is unlike any other type's. And each type reacts according to what he or she sees through that lens.

If you watch the *Feeler, Driver, Analyzer,* or *Elitist* who is close to you, you will notice that the Mood Language each most often uses is that of their Dominant Mood. Even when they are not being rejected, they say things and do things with the speech and body mannerisms of that Dominant Mood.

This chapter gives you the single most important technique of the *3Rs:* the power to tune in directly on another person's Dominant Mood frequency.

## Moderating "Filters": Our Socially Acceptable "Public Faces"

None of us, whatever our personality type, wishes to appear to others as nakedly "Bargaining," "Angry," "Denying," or "Depressed," so we moderate these raw emotions into socially acceptable ones. It is also easier to justify our behavior to ourselves if we can somehow filter out the uncontrolled, "uncivilized" aspects of our natural reactions.

So each personality type subconsciously applies a *filter* over its Dominant Mood to modify and disguise it. The filters of each personality type are:

| Personality Type | Dominant Mood | Filter |
|---|---|---|
| FEELER | Bargaining | Conciliation |
| DRIVER | Anger | Indignation |
| ANALYZER | Denial | Dismissal |
| ELITIST | Depression | Exclusiveness |

The Feeler who, in Bargaining, may be saying at bottom, "Please don't hurt me," now appears, in Conciliation, to be saying, "Let's consider everybody's point of view."

The Driver, who may be nakedly hopping mad, now appears, in Indignation, to be saying, "I'm just annoyed that the world is not the way it should be."

The Analyzer, who in Denial, may be saying, "I'm always

right and everyone else is always wrong," now appears, in Dismissal, to be merely saying, "Well, if you don't want to take my advice, that's your problem."

And the Elitist who, in Depression, believes he or she is deeply misunderstood and unappreciated, now in Exclusiveness, appears to be saying, "You really wouldn't understand what I was talking about anyway, so let's talk about something else you *do* understand."

## "I'VE GOT TO BE ME": OUR OWN UNIQUE VIEW OF THE WORLD

The key to personality types lies in the typical way each uses its Dominant Mood and its superimposed filter.

We do not all see the same "reality." What one person sees in life seems like a "distortion" to another. The way a person of one personality type sees and deals with the experiences of life is very different from the way a person of another personality type would look at and handle similar experiences. What the Feeler, the Driver, the Analyzer, and the Elitist each perceives in the world and what is actually happening in it are very different pictures.

Feelers, in the filtered Mood of Bargaining—*Conciliation*— almost always speak and act politely, with consideration for others' points of view and concern for their emotional comfort. They are always aware of the give-and-take in any situation, and try to right any imbalance of power they feel exists between the people they're with.

---

**conciliation, n.**
the act of conciliating or state of being conciliated.

**conciliate, v.t.**
1. to win over; soothe the anger of; make friendly; placate. 2. to gain (regard, favor, goodwill, esteem, etc.) by friendly acts. 3. to reconcile; make consistent.

*Webster's Unabridged Dictionary* (Second Edition)

---

During his 1992 presidential campaign, Bill Clinton was criticized for not being able to say no to anyone, for hating to alienate anyone, for having a tendency to promise everything to everybody, and for his willingness to conciliate and compromise. He has a reputation as a man who, in his desire to not offend—to be liked—is far too willing to tell people what they want to hear. These are all features of Bargaining.

Critics have said Bill Clinton is this way because of his childhood scars. One person said, "He sat down and walked around, and thought and thought about it, and figured it out. He decided that you ought to go through life not offending anybody." Clinton probably did think about it. But because he is a Feeler, who views his world through the lens of Bargaining, and filters and interprets what he sees there in Conciliation, his "decision" about how he should go through life could not have been other than it is.

In other words, being a Feeler, he saw his world through his Dominant Mood of Bargaining, filtered what he saw through Conciliation, and reacted to it as a Feeler.

Drivers, in the filtered Mood of Anger, usually speak and act quickly and dramatically, "venting" their opinions directly as they almost overwhelmingly take control of the flow and direction of any conversation they have with anyone. They normally react to something they don't think is right with aggressive directness.

---

**indignation, n.**
1. anger mingled with contempt, disgust, or abhorrence, caused by disapprobation of something mean, disgraceful, or unjust. 2. the effects of anger as manifested in judgment or punishment.

**indignant, a.**
to consider as unworthy or improper, to be displeased at; affected with indignation; feeling the mingled emotions of anger and scorn or contempt, as when a person is exasperated by unjust, mean, or ungrateful action or treatment.

*Webster's Unabridged Dictionary* (Second Edition)

As Drivers tend to have set and very definite opinions about most things (the way things ought to be done and said; indeed, the way things *should be*), they become indignant when the world does not conform to their picture of it. And, being Drivers, they air their views about this whether or not you want to hear them. They just cannot resist making a retort. As comedienne Karin Babbitt explains: "You don't want to be rude, but it's a reflex."

They usually have a highly developed sense of humor that, even when it is directed against themselves, is sharp and quick, and is used to demonstrate the absurdity of situations that have aroused their indignation.

Even in Acceptance, Drivers still continue to filter their view of the world through Indignation, judging what they see in terms of "their" ideas of right and wrong, black and white.

Analyzers, in the filtered Mood of Denial, view their world dispassionately, filtering out and dismissing those things that do not make rational sense to them. This "nonsense" has no place in their world—it is irrelevant and not worth the effort of their consideration. The only things that have worth and value to them are those that are coherent, reasonable, rational, and sensible.

---

**dismissal, n.**
1. a dismissing or being dismissed. 2. a notice or order for the dismissing of someone.

**dismiss, v.t.**
1. to send away; to give leave of departure; to permit to depart. 2. to remove or discharge from an office, service, employment, etc. 3. to put out of one's mind. 4. in law, to discontinue or reject (a claim or action) as unworthy of notice or of being granted.

*Webster's Unabridged Dictionary* (Second Edition)

---

An Analyzer friend recounts the story of a duck whose feet were amputated in an accident. A well-known sneaker manufacturer came to the rescue, fitting the duck with prosthetic sneakers so it could waddle about again. A publishing house then commissioned a children's book based on this heart-warming story—but before it could be written, the duck disappeared. Since it was then not possible to photograph the sneakered duck for the book or use it for publicity purposes, the publisher withdrew his offer.

To our friend's mind, this made no sense at all. The logical solution to the problem was obvious: Get another duck, surgically remove its feet under anesthetic, attach another pair of sneakers, and *voilà:* nobody would lose out.

As an Analyzer, she was astonished—and still is—that most people were horrified at the notion. It seemed eminently sensible to her.

Elitists view their world through a tri-focal lens, with a combination of the Conciliation/Indignation/Dismissal filters of the other three personality types. Their view, while being insightful, multifaceted, and "intuitive," frequently becomes distorted by being sifted through such a complex filter.

Because they tend to be more "insightful" than other types, Elitists feel somehow "special" and removed from ordinary run-of-the-mill humanity. They also feel vulnerable to attack and misunderstanding because they are different. So, unless they are with someone very close to them, they rely on elegant role playing to hide their loneliness and depression.

---

**exclusiveness, n.** the quality or state of being exclusive.

**exclusive, a.**
1. excluding all others; shutting out other considerations, happenings, existences, occupations, etc. 2. having the tendency or power to exclude all others. 3. excluding all but what is specified. 4. not shared or divided; sole, single. 5. excluding certain people or groups for social or economic [or intellectual] reasons. 6. snobbish; undemocratic.

*Webster's Unabridged Dictionary* (Second Edition)

Henry Kissinger's latest biographer, Walter Isaacson, says Kissinger's arrogance is "the legacy of a childhood spent feeling both smarter and more beleaguered than those around him." Being an Elitist, whatever his background might have been, he would have been bound to view his world, and himself in it, in this very exclusive way.

## Individual "Triggers": What Sets Us Off

Each personality type has a *trigger* that sets off a reaction. Each type's trigger is distinctive to that personality and is deeply rooted in the particular way it views the world. It is intensely subjective and makes sense only *in its terms.*

Because other personality types do not view the world the same way, and are unaware that any triggering mechanism has even been set off, they are puzzled at the vehemence of the reaction. Because it is not something that would trigger a similar reaction in them, they do not understand what has happened.

The triggers for the personality types are:

| Personality Type | Dominant Mood | Filter | Trigger |
|---|---|---|---|
| FEELER | Bargaining | Conciliation | "Fair/Unfair" |
| DRIVER | Anger | Indignation | "Right/Wrong" |
| ANALYZER | Denial | Dismissal | "Rational"/ "Irrational" |
| ELITIST | Depression | Exclusiveness | "Appropriate/ Inappropriate" |

As long as Feelers see fairness in their view of the world, they will stay in Acceptance. The moment they see *unfairness*

VULNERABLE SELF-IMAGE: THE FEELER
*Dominant Mood: BARGAINING　/　Filter: CONCILIATION　/*

| HAVE AN IMAGE OF THEMSELVES AS BEING: | THEREFORE IN THEIR MOOD LANGUAGE THEY: |
|---|---|
| *Emotionally sensitive* | —think, speak, and act in terms of feelings<br>—try to create empathy and bond<br>—are aware of others' emotional states<br>—are warm, kind, gentle, and polite<br>—are particularly aware of the "feeling tone" of words and actions |
| *Fair and even-handed* | —consider everyone's point of view<br>—listen carefully<br>—need to understand the "full picture"<br>—think and react in a slow, considered way<br>—give others the benefit of the doubt<br>—concede points |
| *Non-aggressive* | —do not push themselves or their opinions<br>—do not try to dominate or control<br>—are patient and non-combative<br>—consider others' needs before their own |
| *Peacemakers who are "good," kind, considerate, and fair* | —try to be diplomatic and tactful, even-handed, non-judgmental, and "peacemaking" |

of any kind, they will react negatively. Their sense of the way things should be has been offended and a reaction has been triggered.

Similarly, Drivers, Analyzers, and Elitists happily remain in Acceptance if they view respectively *their* sense of *right, rational,* or *appropriate* behavior in their pictures of the world. Each of these type's negative reactions are set off by, respectively, *wrong, irrational,* or *inappropriate* behavior because this does not tally with the way they (in their view) think things should be.

*Trigger: "FAIR/UNFAIR"*

|  | THEREFORE REJECTION IS TRIGGERED IF YOU "UNFAIRLY": |
| --- | --- |
|  | —accuse them of being overemotional or emotionally unstable<br>—accuse them of being insensitive or unfeeling<br>—treat them with insensitivity, rudeness, roughness, or insincerity |
|  | —accuse them of being selfish or self-centered<br>—accuse them of being martyrs or letting others walk all over them<br>—accuse them of being slow or indecisive<br>—dismiss their ideas when they do offer an opinion<br>—do not listen with attention and consideration when they are ready to talk or interrupt before they have finished |
|  | —accuse them of being insipid, weak, non-combative, vacillating, or indecisive<br>—try to dominate, control, or aggressively "take charge"<br>—assault them with anger, loudness, rudeness, or any form of force<br>—treat them with impatience or constantly interrupt or talk over them |
|  | —devalue—even indirectly—their sense of "goodness," kindness, consideration, and fairness |

## The "Tender Spot"

Each personality type has a corresponding "tender spot," which you must be very careful not to hit, graze, or even gently touch.

This tender spot is the vulnerable underbelly of people's image of themselves. That image of themselves is a combination of their own sense of value, worth, merit, and "character"—it is what they believe makes them "lovable" to you.

VULNERABLE SELF-IMAGE: THE DRIVER
*Dominant Mood: ANGER   /   Filter: INDIGNATION   /*

| HAVE AN IMAGE OF THEMSELVES AS BEING: | THEREFORE IN THEIR MOOD LANGUAGE THEY: |
|---|---|
| *Passionately enthusiastic* | —think, speak, and act assertively<br>—try to orchestrate what is happening so that it can all happen the "right" way<br>—play to "an audience" and manipulate it dramatically into agreement with jumps from one aspect of the subject to another<br>—say the same thing over and over until they get their audience to "react"<br>—become indignant if things do not go the "right" way |
| *Quick thinking* | —think and react rapidly (bore easily, react impatiently)<br>—draw conclusions and make decisions quickly, then act purposefully to carry them through to a conclusion<br>—savor intellectual and emotional "game playing"<br>—jump from subject to subject and change thought direction abruptly<br>—react admiringly and enjoy sparring with worthy opponents who can keep up with them<br>—bore easily and react impatiently to subjects that do not interest them |
| *Sharp-thinking and percepetive* | —believe and trust only their own perceptions, are skeptical of other's views, and react indignantly if they do not accord with their own<br>—are definite, direct, and confident about what they think |
| *Sidewalk superintendents who know how things should be done* | —try to manipulate others into seeing and doing things the "right" way |

If you inadvertently or carelessly devalue that image, they think you are devaluing them, belittling their worth, and rejecting the very core of the person you claim to love.

*Trigger: "RIGHT/WRONG"*

| THEREFORE REJECTION IS TRIGGERED IF YOU "WRONGLY": |
| --- |
| —refuse to play the game by their rules<br>—fail to react enthusiastically or passionately enough<br>—appear to lose interest or become bored or dismissive of them and their views<br>—as an unworthy opponent, dare to try to usurp control and dominate, and fail to bring it off<br>(Drivers do not suffer fools gladly: they do not suffer them at all) |
| —refuse to or are unable to keep up with them<br>—bore them<br>—ignore them<br>—dismiss them |
| —challenge their perceptions or their opinions<br>—force them to see themselves in any terms other than their own<br>—treat their opinions with derision |
| —devalue or belittle who and what they believe they are |

The four charts beginning on page 142 pinpoint those tender spots in the vulnerable self-image of the personality types, together with the kind of "mistreatment" that will trigger their rejection of you.

VULNERABLE SELF-IMAGE: THE ANALYZER
*Dominant Mood: DENIAL  /  Filter: DISMISSAL  /*

| HAVE AN IMAGE OF THEMSELVES AS BEING: | THEREFORE IN THEIR MOOD LANGUAGE THEY: |
|---|---|
| *Sensible and level-headed* | —are serious-minded and stable<br>—remain cool-headed, unflappable, and do not get side-tracked<br>—keep a tight rein on their emotions, to a point of sometimes appearing completely emotionally detached or "wooden"<br>—react uncomfortably to anything smacking of frivolity or "silliness"<br>—find it difficult to laugh at themselves |
| *Rational and clear-sighted* | —think, act, and speak clearly, succinctly, and analytically<br>—draw conclusions solely from the facts in a precise, ordered manner<br>—react to situations in terms of what is for and against them personally, what can and cannot be used to their advantage<br>—move unerringly and systematically to their "bottom line"<br>—consider anything irrational or emotional unimportant and a waste of time |
| *Direct and straightforward* | —think, act, and speak directly, assertively, and without artifice or "polite" consideration for others' feelings<br>—see their opinions and behavior as the only obviously rational way to think and behave and reject any challenge to their way of thinking with contempt<br>—refuse ever to admit they could be wrong or at fault unless the evidence to the contrary is logically incontrovertible<br>—can become extremely opinionated, dogmatic, or arrogant in asserting their correctness |
| *Decision makers who are always on target in the planning and execution of whatever they set out to achieve* | —assess everything with a structured, focused precision and work out how it can be used advantageously |

*Trigger: "LOGICAL/ILLOGICAL"*

| THEREFORE REJECTION IS TRIGGERED IF YOU "ILLOGICALLY": |
| --- |
| —approach them playfully with teasing or bantering "nonsense"<br>—display, become affected by, or be motivated by, excessive emotion<br>—accuse them of being overly serious, cold, inhuman, or callous |
| —waste their time with meandering, unfocused comments or ideas<br>—talk to them in emotional terms<br>—accuse them of being selfish and only seeing the world in terms of what they can get out of it<br>—accuse them of being heartless or devoid of any human feeling |
| —criticize them<br>—try to force them to see their faults in any terms other than their own reasoning, logical way<br>—attempt to control or dominate them |
| —devalue or belittle who and what they believe they are |

VULNERABLE SELF-IMAGE: THE ELITIST
*Dominant Mood: DEPRESSION   /   Filter: EXCLUSIVENESS   /*

| HAVE AN IMAGE OF THEMSELVES AS BEING: | THEREFORE IN THEIR MOOD LANGUAGE THEY: |
|---|---|
| *Intellectually powerful* | —think, act, and speak with intellectual sophistication and style<br>—are mentally (and emotionally) restless, always searching for new and fertile concepts to explore<br>—grasp whole concepts rapidly and see "grand" solutions insightfully<br>—are always mindful of future repercussions and want to solve problems and get results here and now<br>—react with impatience and condescension when what they say goes over others' heads |
| *Superior, "one-of-a-kind"* | —take charge, dominating and controlling people and situations with their presence and style<br>—project their egos, and give the impression the whole world revolves around them<br>—evince little real feeling for others and do not even attempt to bond on any but a superficial "polite" level<br>—display impeccable manners, charm, and taste |
| *Deep and complex* | —remain distant, aloof and "alone," convinced they will never find a kindred soul with the ability to understand them.<br>—cloak their real feelings in mannered role playing<br>—feel as a "minority of one" insecure and vulnerable to attack and misunderstanding<br>—constantly hint at a deep personal sense of underlying depression, disappointment, and melancholia |
| *Visionary thinkers, able to go directly and intuitively to the heart of the matter* | —dominate by the sense of their natural superiority and sense of aristocratic aloofness |

*Trigger: "APPROPRIATE/INAPPROPRIATE"*

| THEREFORE REJECTION IS TRIGGERED IF YOU "INAPPROPRIATELY": |
| --- |
| —fail to treat them with due respect<br>—have the impertinence to approach them on an equal footing in an intellectually unsound, unfocused, and "fuzzy" manner<br>—appear merely to want to discuss or review a problem and not actually solve it on the spot<br>—puncture their balloon by dismissing or doubting the worth of their overall grand scheme of things |
| —impertinently try to control, lead, or guide them to your way of thinking<br>—offer advice to them<br>—give the impression you consider yourself their equal<br>—approach them in a coarse, common, boorish, or loutish manner<br>—attempt to be overly familiar and "pally" |
| —attempt to give the impression you do understand them, when clearly you don't<br>—as their choice of intimate, fail to understand that their Depression is a bonding mechanism with you, and betray them by dismissing, ignoring, or failing to realize its significance |
| —devalue and belittle who and what they believe they are |

Now that you are aware of what triggers rejection in each of the personality types, you know what to avoid doing and saying.

There is, however, one more vitally important technique to learn, which draws all your knowledge together and makes it work in your favor, and that is what actually to *do* to get through—directly—to the person you so desperately want to reach.

## SPEAKING ANOTHER'S LANGUAGE: HOW TO TUNE IN ON EACH PERSONALITY TYPE'S MOOD FREQUENCY

Being actually able to speak another person's Mood Language is the single most important skill that you can learn from this book.

It allows you to speak *directly* to who they are, in a way they will understand immediately, clearly, and unequivocally.

With this technique, you are in fact "tuning in" on their wavelength and speaking directly to their *subconscious* way of thinking and feeling.

They do not have to "interpret" or "translate" what you say into their terms because you are already clearly speaking in their terms. They do not have to take the time, make the effort, or even try to understand your meaning because your meaning is obvious—it is how they understand meaning anyway.

In the children's tale *The Snow Queen,* the heroine, Gerda, is trying desperately to find her friend. Her search leads her through a forest where she meets a raven. Gerda asks the raven if he knows where her friend has gone, and the raven replies, "I'll tell you . . . but if only you understood raven speech I could tell you better."

The technique of tuning in on another person's Mood Frequency gives you the power not only to understand "raven speech" but to speak it yourself. This technique gives you the ability to speak fluent "Feeler," "Driver," "Analyzer," and "Elitist" speech.

The following four charts on how to tune in on each personality type's Dominant Mood Frequency give you the rules to follow to speak another person's language. Commit them to memory, and try to use them every time you talk with the people who are important in your life.

It is essential, however, that you use each and every one of these rules without fail when you respond to a person who is rejecting of you. You will not be able to lead that person smoothly through to Acceptance or on to Mutual Acceptance if you do not apply these rules.

If you follow these rules, people you are trying to guide will not only be in Acceptance but will remain in it, and will be genuinely open to any idea you care to put to them. They will receive your signals loud and clear—on their wavelength— without any of the distortion caused by crossed signals.

### HOW TO TUNE IN ON A FEELER'S "MOOD FREQUENCY"

Speak to them in terms of feelings
  —even their logic is based in emotion
Be sensitive to their physical reactions
  —they are unable to hide minute emotional leakages of Mood
  Language
Be gentle, polite, and empathetic
Lower your voice and slow your speech
Present one idea at a time
  —they are processing the complete picture
Do not try to dominate, control, or force them into anything
  —anger, loudness, abrasiveness, theatrics, or any form of ex-
  treme behavior will make them close off and shut you out
Be patient and never rush them or interrupt their pauses or si-
    lences
  —they are intellectually mediating
Ask them directly what they think
  —they rarely volunteer their opinions
Above all, *listen* when they talk. They have carefully considered
    what they think and usually have sound, fair solutions,
      which take account of your needs even more than their own

--------

**Feelers,** in the spirit of Bargaining and Conciliation, are happy
    if they get 80% of what they want. However, if you give
    them 100% of what they want, they feel the scales of give-
    and-take have been unfairly weighted in their favor and
    they will not rest easy until they have "repaid" you tenfold.

### How to Tune In on a Driver's "Mood Frequency"

Be wholehearted in everything you say and do
  —they need to see dramatic, enthusiastic reactions
Speed up your thought processes and speak more quickly
  —keep up with them
Talk in concrete, not abstract, terms. Use examples from real situations to prove your point or back up your opinion
  —they will dismiss anything that is not based in reality
Be direct and succinct and get to the point
  —they will stop listening if you are long-winded
Be assertive, do not back down or give in
  —they will consider you weak and an unworthy opponent
Always allow them to control the direction and flow of the conversation, unless you are very sure you can wrest it from them and win all the ensuing verbal skirmishes it will cost to hold it (in which case you will win their admiration)
Above all, *enjoy* their vitality and strength of purpose, and become part of it. Their perceptiveness usually does allow them to draw the right conclusions and come up with the right solutions, even if their way of getting you to see it with them can be overwhelming

————

**Drivers,** in the spirit of passionate enthusiasm, *need* things to go 100% their way. However, if you give them this 100% as passionately and enthusiastically as they feel it should be given, there is a very good chance that they will passionately and enthusiastically give it right back to you to prove you can't outdo them.

---

**HOW TO TUNE IN ON AN ANALYZER'S "MOOD FREQUENCY"**

Be calm and composed mentally, emotionally, and physically
—they cannot relate to agitated, frenetic, or overly dramatic
thoughts, emotions, or behavior

Concentrate your mental abilities, organize and structure your
thoughts, and be focused and directed when speaking
—they will become impatient and dismiss anything you have
to say otherwise

Present your ideas precisely and succinctly in the form of facts,
not opinions, which are either for or against them
—they will deflect, and at times not even "hear," anything not
presented to them this way

Never speak in emotional terms or show your feelings
—they view this as a weakness, with no logical validity or
worth

Never criticize them
—they have no ability to pass judgment on themselves and are
genuinely confused by such attacks

Do not confront them, dominate them, or try to take control, unless you are very sure you can change their minds

Above all, appreciate, give them credit for, and take advantage
of their rationality and clearsightedness

Their logical abilities allow them to get to the heart of the matter and make things work

---

## How to Tune In on an Elitist's "Mood Frequency"

Treat them with respect and due deference
   —they need you to understand that they are special
Never try to dominate or control them
   —they will never accept that you are of superior, or even
   equal, rank
Be clear-thinking and focused when talking to them on any
      subject
   —they will treat even minor lapses with total dismissive contempt
See the "big picture"
   —details are only important insofar as they are a means to an
   end
See the big picture from every perspective: intellectual and emo-
      tional, theoretical and practical, personal and impersonal
   —they can process and appreciate anything that is put to them
   in the right way
Never be impolite, crass, ill-mannered, or inappropriate
   —they will, politely, and in a very well-mannered, well-bred
   way, cut you off at the knees
If you love them and if you want them to love you, always, al-
      ways bond with their Depression
   —it is their way of sharing themselves with you
Above all, appreciate the fact that the Elitist personality is a combination of all the other personality types (Feeler, Driver, and Analyzer) and that—if you can bear with them—like a warp-speed
ride on the U.S.S. *Enterprise* in "Star Trek," they may take you
where no other person has gone before

NINE

# How to Keep People in Acceptance

Now that you have the person closest to you in Acceptance, here are some additional ways of *keeping* him or her there.

## STAY TUNED IN ON THEIR MOOD FREQUENCY: SPEAK THEIR LANGUAGE

Follow the rules on how to get through and reach all of the personality types in their own terms, and adapt your own natural Mood Frequency to suit theirs.

If, for example, they are a Driver type and you're a Feeler, talk and think in "Driver" terms; or if you are a Driver and they are a Feeler, talk and think in "Feeler" terms.

## REINFORCE THEIR OWN IMAGE OF THEMSELVES

In terms of their personality type, show you love, admire, and approve of those things they think they're good at.

These may not be the things about them that you really do love and admire and approve of (what you, with your personality type, love, admire, and approve of about them may be totally different), but *they* think they are. Since you are responding to them *in their terms,* those are the things you should focus on.

Keep in mind that even if what you are saying sounds artificial and "phoney" to you, it will not sound that way to them. To them it will sound like exactly what they always hoped to hear from someone.

Clearly, the following general purpose guidelines are somewhat artificial. You should vary them to suit your style of conversation, the person you're speaking to, and the specific circumstances of the conversation itself.

Try out any version of these image-reinforcing stamps of approval and watch the positively amazing response they elicit.

### What to Say and Who to Say It To

*Say to the FEELER (warmly):*
"What I like about you most is the way you're always so thoughtful toward other people. You always try so hard not to hurt their feelings and to treat them with consideration— even when sometimes maybe they don't really deserve it.

"You never try to control other people or dominate them. You always listen to what they have to say and treat it with respect.

"You never rush in the way other people do and make decisions without knowing all the facts. You consider every aspect of the situation carefully before you come to a decision.

"You always seem to care so much for everyone else that sometimes it worries me a little. Maybe just once or twice you ought to think of your own interests first."

*Say to the DRIVER (wholeheartedly):*
"What I like about you the most is the way you always get so passionately enthusiastic and involved in things.

"If there's a problem to be dealt with, I can always rely on you to deal with it quickly and efficiently. You seem to be able to make a hundred decisions all at once—and every one of them is the right one.

"You always say you're not working as hard as you should be, but you work harder than anyone I know. Everything you do, you do thoroughly and properly, but at the same time with such verve and flair.

"And I particularly admire you for always being your own man (woman). You're never a follower, always a leader."

### Say to the ANALYZER (seriously):

"What I like about you most is that you're always so cool-headed in a crisis. You always have everything—including yourself—totally under control. I know I can always rely on you to work things out properly.

"I love the way you fight for what you believe in; you never back down from anything. And you never lie or try to sugar-coat the truth—you always say exactly what you think.

"You're so systematic and focused in everything you do—no wonder you always come out on top.

"And I really admire the way you take in the most complicated and involved ideas so patiently, and then make such simple, logical, and perfect sense out of them."

### Say to the ELITIST (respectfully):

"What I like about you most is that you have a way of making things happen that no one else has.

"You really are the most exciting and intellectually stimulating person I've ever met. You have such presence and style in everything you do.

"No wonder you always come out on top—you have such a unique and insightful way of getting right to the heart of everything.

"You are the most genuinely charismatic person I've ever known."

## "I'LL JUST SIT HERE": POSITION YOURSELF FOR MAXIMUM EFFECT

All people tend to focus their attention physically to one particular side, whether right or left. From that angle and perspective they are happier and more comfortable dealing with other people, or merely taking in information.

Which side they favor depends on which side of their brain they use most. The right side of the brain houses intuition, emotion, and motor skills, while the left side controls cognitive functioning. The right brain processes a wide variety of visual, emotional, and sensory information as an overall picture; the left brain organizes separate facts sequentially and logically.

Although we all use both hemispheres of our brains, we were all born with one side dominant. Despite learning to use the functions of both sides to get us through life, repeated use of our dominant side has become a habit. When we role-play at being someone else, we call on our whole brain for "whole-life learning." But when we settle into "being ourselves," or when stress forces us to retreat into our core personality, we return to the side of the brain we feel most at home in.

The left brain controls functions on the right side of the body and the right brain controls functions on the left side of the body.

*Feelers,* who are most comfortable using their right brain, where they can decide how they "feel" about things, will always, when pondering about something using that side of the brain, look to the left. When they break eye contact, this is the direction they have a habit of glancing in.

So, if you want to get a Feeler's full attention, sit or stand slightly to their left.

Feelers, in Acceptance, do not mind your moving in very close to them, so position yourself carefully a little to their left and maintain an easy, undominating eye contact with them to assure them of your interest.

*Analyzers,* who are far more at ease using their left brain, where they can "analyze" facts in a precise, structured, rational manner, will always, when processing ideas using that side of the brain, look to the right. When they glance away, this is the direction they usually look in.

So, if you want an Analyzer's complete attention, sit or stand slightly to their right.

Even when in acceptance, Analyzers control their emotional responses to intimacy, so do not get too close to them unless you know from experience that they will be emotionally responsive to close contact. Maintain always-attentive eye contact with them, and nod from time to time to show you are following their logic.

*Drivers,* who skip back and forth in both sides of their quick brains, settle into predominantly left-brain thinking when in Acceptance or great stress. While they process information rapidly in both emotional and cognitive terms, the final arbiter is the left, fact-analysis hemisphere; so they glance to their right most frequently.

To hold a Driver's undivided attention, sit or stand slightly to their right.

Being enthusiastic, dramatic people, Drivers appreciate animation in others, so your distance from them can be varied for effect and to stop them from getting bored. Maintain a bright and alert eye contact with them, using the guidelines for How to Tune In on a Driver's Mood Frequency (p. 153), and you will have an immediate impact on them.

*Elitists,* who can think and feel in the manner of all the other three types, use both sides of their brains. Their method of thought processing is a "fusion" of the methods used by the other types, which gives them a greater overall insight.

When in great stress, Elitists have only two gears: fast forward or fast reverse (great Anger or great Depression). But Elitists in acceptance become more emotionally and rationally "moderate," and less obviously "personality typecast" than any of the other types.

With the Elitist, you may position yourself anywhere you feel comfortable. But watch their eye movements carefully, and if you can detect any predominant direction of movement, stand or sit in line with it.

## KNOW WHEN AND IF TO TOUCH

Once people are in Acceptance, they are ready to "share" themselves with you, and sharing flows more easily and naturally between two people who are touching. Two people physically "in touch" with each other relieve each other's feelings of separateness and loneliness. They generate feelings of comfort, reassurance, protection, and love.

It has also been found that if you touch people when you ask them to do something, they are far more likely to comply.

However, each personality type reacts differently to being touched, both among mere acquaintances and with people they know and care for.

When among acquaintances, **Feelers** have little objection to being touched socially by non-threatening strangers and acquaintances, but **Drivers** object strenuously to this type of contact and prefer to keep their distance. **Analyzers,** who do not attach any particular emotional significance to social touching, do not care one way or the other. And **Elitists,** being aloof, will condone social touching only when it is appropriate.

Yet, when they are with people who are important to them, the personality types behave differently again. **Feelers,** at the very onset of stress in an argument, must not be touched.

They require time to consider their feelings, without the interference or coercion of close contact.

*Drivers,* on the other hand, at the very onset of stress in an argument can be defused instantaneously and brought straight into Acceptance with a wholehearted hug and a direct, heartfelt apology. Try it with the Driver in your life. It works wonders.

When *Analyzers* are with people they love and trust, they no longer feel the need to control their emotions, and they take real delight in touching and being touched.

In private with the one person they want to open up to, *Elitists* derive an enormous sense of comfort and reassurance from being touched.

With all personality types in Acceptance, there are certain non-verbal Mood Language signals that are a direct appeal for touching. When you see a cluster of any two or more of the following, move in close to the person you care for and either touch them lightly or embrace them gently:

- They turn one or both of their hands palm upward in their lap.
- Their palm is turned outward as they stroke their hair back away from their face. (Usually a female signal)
- They cry.
- Their lips change color as they purse their upper and lower lips together for between 15 to 30 seconds.
- Their chin drops to their throat and they let out a large, audible sigh.
- They drop and round both of their shoulders.
- Their hand rubs at the bottom part of their chin while they hold a smile on their face.
- Their eyes look upward as an exaggerated, slow blinking process begins.
- They physically "reach out" for you or touch you.

You will know from experience what type of touching the people who are important to you are most responsive to. Read their reactions carefully and note especially whether or not they are reciprocating your touch. If they are not, back off slightly. They will let you know when they are ready to "share" themselves.

## REMEMBER WHO THEY ARE AND WHO YOU ARE

Remember that all four of the personality types process the same information in very different ways.

*Feelers* consider the whole picture. They take everything into account, slowly and carefully; weave it all together so that it makes sense in their terms; and then consider how they "feel" about it.

*Drivers* immediately extract what they consider to be the essential features; lose interest in anything else; and judge whether it is right or wrong in their terms.

*Analyzers* extract the facts; put them together systematically; and draw a rational conclusion in terms of what is for or against them.

*Elitists* do all of the above.

This has been taken into account in the guidelines on How to Tune In on Mood Frequencies, but when you are concentrating on *keeping* those closest to you in Acceptance, remember not to slip back into presenting your ideas and thoughts in your way. Use *their* language.

## "DO YOU SEE WHAT I HEAR?": USE THE OTHER PERSON'S VISUAL AND AUDITORY WAYS OF PROCESSING INFORMATION

While all of us use all of our senses—sight, sound, touch, and taste—to process information, some people rely primarily on visual images, while others rely mainly on auditory input.

Where one person may take in information as a series of pictures or visual images, another may take it in as a series of sounds, tones, or auditory notes.

To determine where they place most reliance, ask them to describe an enjoyable time they had at, say, the beach, and see if they describe it in terms of what they saw or in terms of what they heard. (For example, whether they recollect the *sight* or the *sound* of the surf breaking on the sand.)

If they use visual images, always talk to them in terms of pictures. If they use auditory images, always speak to them about everything in terms of sound.

This *visual* or *auditory imaging* is independent of personality type, and you can use it to enhance the clarity and sharpness of your communication with any type, further deepening their feeling of Acceptance.

All that remains now, once we have gotten the people closest, nearest—and perhaps dearest—to us to accept the fact that we love them, is to demonstrate just how we would like them, in turn, to love us. We can do this by using the last, and perhaps most satisfying, of the *3Rs—Reciprocation.*

## Yawning

Webster's dictionary defines the verb "to yawn" as:
  *v.i.* to open the mouth wide, especially involuntarily, and with a deep inhalation, as a result of fatigue, drowsiness, or boredom.

However, this definition is not quite complete. People, especially those under thirty, also yawn as a result of stress. They do it to release tension.

A child, being scolded at length by an adult, and unable to vent her frustration and anger at such "injustice" by fidgeting or answering back, will often (apparently inappropriately) let out a huge yawn. The greater her stress, the more extreme her yawn: sometimes with an exaggerated shuddering of the whole body.

Young adults, in difficult, confrontational periods of their relationships, may suddenly start yawning more frequently than is normal in order to relieve the tension of their pent-up feelings.

So, if your partner starts yawning at what appears to you to be the wrong moment, don't assume he or she is merely tired or bored: there is more to a "yawn" than that.

*Webster's Unabridged Dictionary* (Second Edition)

## A Note on Crying

Women cry more often than men.

They need to.

Stress in women causes a build-up of prolactin and adrenocorticotropic hormones, which are actually physically released in the shedding of tears.

Until puberty, boys and girls cry equally as often; after puberty, when males and females respond to different hormonal influences, female blood levels of prolactin are 60% higher than those of the male.

A woman in stress gains emotional relief by spontaneously flushing out the unhealthy excesses of chemicals and hormones through tears of anger or sadness or joy. A man, who has no such build-up to relieve, sheds his tears only under enormous distress.

So, in any relationship between a man and a woman, it is no use suggesting to the man that he learn to express his "emotional sensitivity" by crying more.

Unlike a woman, he simply *can't.*

# PART THREE

# "READ, RESPOND, AND RECIPROCATE"

TEN

# The Steps of Reciprocation

Loving—as any schoolboy and schoolgirl smitten with a hopeless and unrequited crush will tell you—is not enough. We need love returned.

All human beings yearn to be loved, understood, and validated.

It is all very well understanding other people deeply because we love them, but we are, at base, also doing this so we can get the person we love to understand us deeply in return. We all suffer from the Bargaining need to exclaim: "What about *me?* Where's *my* fair share?"

So far, in our efforts to *Read* and *Respond* to the people we love, we have neutralized our own moods and concentrated on tuning in on their Mood Frequency—we have kept who and what we are under firm control for their sake.

But so far only half of *us* has been loved and understood.

Sooner or later, depending on our personality type, we begin to think and feel that this continued onesidedness is ei-

169

ther "unfair," "wrong," "irrational," or "inappropriate," and our own rejection trigger starts quivering.

*We* now want to be understood and loved for who and what we are. We want the person we have spent so much time considering to realize that we see the world very differently from them, and that the way we see it is as justified and deserving of understanding as theirs is.

We not only want this—we long for it. We long to be loved *on our terms,* responded to on *our* Mood Frequency, and have our needs met and satisfied in *our* way. We want them to see why we do and say things the way we do. We don't want to be "forgiven" or even "have allowances made" for thinking and feeling, doing and saying things differently from them. We want who and what we are to be understood, accepted, and approved. And we want them to love us for *who and what we really are.*

Having followed the *Read* and *Respond* stages, we have learned how to love them. Now we need them to learn how to love us in *Reciprocation.*

Yet how do we begin to get them to love us in the same genuine and understanding way we have learned to love them, and to appreciate the differences between us?

## DIFFERENT WORLDS, ALIEN LANDSCAPES: TRYING TO "CHANGE PLACES" WITH EACH OTHER

Before we can get other people to love and accept us fully, we have to bring them to an awareness of just how fundamental the differences between us are.

We must show them that the reason they do and say things differently from us is because they *think* and *feel* differently. We must get them to understand that each of us always has—and always will have—a different way of seeing the world and reacting to it.

We know that they can never put themselves in our place

and see the world through our mind's eye, any more than we can put ourself in their place. However, just as we have learned to understand how they see their world through the lens of their Dominant Mood, we can show them how we see *ours*.

Doing this is not just a matter of "changing places," even if it is done with goodwill and shared empathy. One of the techniques of marriage counseling is to ask each spouse to imagine him- or herself in the other's place and ask, "If I were this person, what would I be thinking about? How would I be feeling? What would I be wishing? What would I be thinking about doing? What conflicts would I be experiencing?"

This is one of the most common techniques, and a basic rubric of marriage counseling that works sometimes—but only when the two partners are the same personality type, view the world through the same Dominant Mood and its filter, and are almost identical save for their sex.

However, as we have seen, an attraction between two identical personality types is not common but rare. What usually faces any (even the best-intentioned) marriage counselor may be not two perfect personality "clones," but two highly individual and different, warring people who do not understand each other at all. Two separate people who cannot possibly think, feel, or experience the same thing in the same way. So any bland, general purpose reconciliation method based on an all-encompassing technique for all seasons is not going to work.

For this simple reason alone, counseling—like the marriages it attempts to heal—breaks down again and again.

## Carl and Suzanne: The Analyzer and the Feeler

A married couple, Carl and Suzanne, spent six months in counseling trying to work out their problems before their inevitable tragic divorce. Individually, each is a good friend and a pleasure to be with. As a married couple, they turned into a disaster to themselves and to everyone who knew them.

Carl is an Analyzer who is urbane, charming, and an engrossing conversationalist, with sharp intelligence and an endless store of amusing anecdotes.

Suzanne, who is a Feeler, is well educated, highly sophisticated, naturally kind and thoughtful, and has a warm graciousness that puts everyone around her at ease.

When they met, he was a well-known sportswriter and she was an established sports-equipment design engineer. They seemed a perfect match: his precise, straightforward manner was softened by contact with her gentler, more considerate approach to life, and her occasionally somewhat abstract way of thinking was sharpened and honed by his tougher, more concrete style of thinking.

Separately, they were both highly attractive people, stimulating and fun to be with. Their friends could not have been happier when they married.

Almost immediately after the marriage, they both decided to resign from their old jobs and set up an exercise and aerobics gym—one of their mutual passions—so that they could not only live together but work together as well.

For the first few years, while they were struggling to make the business a commercial success—and working eighteen hours a day on almost nothing else—their relationship and love for each other remained rock solid. Carl worked out the logistics of setting up the gym, handled the financing, and did the equipment buying and maintenance; Suzanne handled the public relations, advertising, and staff hiring.

Carl loved the way Suzanne managed (by using a warm, empathetic, understanding tone in the advertising) to attract a previously untapped clientele, which would normally be too embarrassed to use a gym. And she had hired staff who were remarkably loyal and had a wonderful knack of keeping the clients so pleased with the atmosphere in the gym, they not only kept coming back but introduced growing numbers of their friends.

Suzanne loved the way Carl managed (with such clear-sighted planning and smooth efficiency) to get the business up and running so quickly and put them into profit in such a surprisingly short time.

It seemed to everyone that the two were on the path to riches and success. And they were: the gym made money and they were able to employ a manager and cut their workload in half so they could relax and enjoy more of each other's company.

It was then that the first cracks in their relationship began to show. While they had been working eighteen hours a day, engrossed (virtually autonomously) in making their own side of the business run smoothly, they had loved, respected, and admired each other. However, once they had the leisure to step out of their own areas of expertise and look more closely at what each had been doing and the way he or she had been doing it, the problems started.

Carl thought Suzanne was too "soft" on the staff: she didn't dock their pay when they were occasionally late; she gave them valuable time to do holiday shopping, attend their kids' school concerts or sports events; and she seemed unable to control the (to his mind) increasingly overfamiliar attitude they were adopting. He also had complaints about the length of time she spent with clients.

Suzanne, for her part, thought Carl was too "cold and calculating" in the way he handled the suppliers; she felt he was penny-pinching in a way that would ruin all the goodwill she had built up; and she objected to his (to her mind) abrasive, uncaring attitude toward her staff.

At this juncture, for the first time they began grating on each other another. They started pounding at each other's "tender spot" and triggering painfully unexpected responses.

Because of Carl's inherently more assertive and straightforward personality, he would say exactly what he thought and, without realizing it, hurt Suzanne's feelings deeply. She felt he was being "unfair" and attacking her personally.

Given Suzanne's essentially non-confrontational, more conciliatory stance, she felt unable to stand up to Carl. So she would attack him in a roundabout way, obliquely letting him know how she felt about what he was doing. He could not really see what she was getting at. He thought she was being "irrational" and attacking him personally.

Gradually, Carl's views on how things should be done began to dominate as he took over more and more control not only in the business but in their personal lives. Suzanne felt increasingly dominated and unempowered, and took her frustrations out on him. She also began to look for understanding and warmth from some of the male trainers at the gym, spending more time with them.

Both were miserable, each feeling deeply misunderstood and wronged. They argued incessantly in private and, despite their efforts to keep up appearances, it began to become obvious to their friends.

Things came to a disastrous head about a year later at a party for Carl's birthday when a friend gave him a battered antique backgammon board he had found at a flea market. Carl, addicted to the game, which he played with an intensity and seriousness (to Suzanne) out of proportion to the fifty-cent bets he played for, was absolutely thrilled at such a considerate gift. Holding up the board in one hand, and the expensive silk shirts Suzanne had given him in the other, as if balancing them both on an imaginary scale, Carl announced, "Now this is a *real* gift! Why can't you give me something like this?"

Despite her suddenly frozen smile, and the acute embarrassment of many of the guests, Carl was totally unaware that he had humiliated Suzanne deeply—and irreconcilably—in front of all their friends.

After that incident, she closed herself off from him completely. Their marriage was over. It was only with reluctance that Suzanne agreed to one last-ditch effort, to see if they could salvage any of what they had once had together through the help of a professional marriage guidance counselor.

## THE FALLACY OF TRYING TO BECOME EACH OTHER: WHY MARRIAGE COUNSELING OFTEN FAILS

In their first marriage counseling session, Suzanne and Carl were told to put themselves in each other's place in a reenactment of the birthday party incident that had so upset Suzanne.

She was asked to repeat the words: "Now this is a *real* gift! Why can't you give me something like this?" exactly the way Carl had said them.

In repeating the words, she changed them subtly: "Now *this* is a real gift! Why can't *you* [ever] give me [anything] like this?" somehow managing to make it sound as if he had been accusing her in a vicious way of being thoughtless, cheap, uncaring, mean-spirited.

Carl was astonished at this interpretation.

Then he was asked to repeat the words the way he had said them so that Suzanne could put herself in his place. He repeated them as if they were merely an objective, impersonal analysis on the merits of two gifts.

She was horrified at this view. But he could not understand why.

The marriage counselor then explained that they were both still being themselves. For the therapy to work properly, they had to try to "become" each other, they had to role-play at being the other person in order to experience each other's feelings: Suzanne had to "feel" the way Carl had when she spoke his words, and Carl had to "feel" Suzanne's reaction on hearing them.

But however hard they tried not to put their own spin on each other's actions, deep down neither one could really believe that there was no malice or ill-intent.

Logically, it made no sense to Carl—what he had done was merely state a fact. It had been the truth. Compared to the shirts, the backgammon board *was* a manifestly better choice of gift. How could anyone be offended by the stating of an obvious fact? He was irritated at Suzanne's overemotional response and thought she was just being silly.

While he conceded that, knowing her as he did, he should have realized that sort of comment would have upset her, he could no more put himself in her place than she could put herself in his.

Suzanne, the Feeler, with her profound sensitivity to emotional rather than rational sense, could never do the 180-degree turn it would require to see all this in Carl's terms.

Nevertheless, in the hope that they would eventually gain some insight into the real cause of the growing chasm between them, the couple continued to attend counseling sessions for six months, assiduously reversing roles, taking part in empathetic discussions, giving each other "breathing space," expressing their "inner selves," taking turns at doing what the other wanted, and even playing sexual games.

It did no lasting good. Finally, they agreed to free each other from their intense individual loneliness within the relationship and end the marriage.

### We Alone Can Share Who We Are with the Person We Love

Without a thorough understanding of each other's vastly different personality traits and their almost contradictory Dominant Moods, Carl and Suzanne could never hope to see

each other as being anything but perversely "unfair"/"irrational" and cruel.

So how could a stranger, albeit a well-intentioned and
practiced professional, hope to get each to see into and understand the very wellsprings of the other's differences? The
counselor himself, without understanding those basic differences, seeing and judging two people through his own Dominant Mood and filter, could never show them how to rediscover what it was they loved about each other.

They had to do it themselves, just as—in the real world—
we all must.

No one, trained or otherwise, knows intimately who we really are but us. And no one but us can explain who we really
are to the person we love. No one else knows our most intimate fears, our most secret insecurities, our hidden inadequacies, or our deepest needs, yearnings, hopes, and dreams.
Yet we cannot (and will not) share this deepest part of who
we believe we are unless we feel we can trust the person we
love to understand us *in our own terms.*

In other words, we need them to be able to visualize what
our world looks like through our lens and—*from that viewpoint*—to understand the way we are, and why we do and say
the things we do and say. We want them to see that we may
not be the person they have always believed us to be, a re-
flection of them, but a person in our own right—complex, singular, different, individual, and above all, separate.

For a full, deep, truly reciprocal relationship, we need them
to love us for who we *really* are.

This *Reciprocation*—the third and perhaps most important
of the *3Rs*—is the key to true mutual understanding and love.

When we were developing the techniques of the *3Rs* we
asked Carl and Suzanne, then divorced for two years, if they
were interested in trying out and testing the techniques. They

both agreed. But, still bitter and hurting, both preferred to learn about the *3Rs* separately.

As Carl and Suzanne became familiar with their own and each other's personality types (Analyzer and Feeler) and understood how the lenses of their respective Dominant Moods (Denial and Bargaining) explained so much about them they had never understood before, they gained new insight into both themselves and each other.

Both saw how each had been assuming the other was merely a slightly off-key version of the other. Each had arrogantly taken for granted that the other thought and felt the same way he/she did.

Things they had said and done to each other, which had caused so much pain, resentment, and distrust, they now realized were never intended that way. Suddenly the assumptions they had made that the other person was being thoughtless, selfish, inconsiderate, or just downright mean-spirited seemed quite unfounded.

They found they were developing new respect for each other, and in the process were rekindling feelings they both thought were long dead.

Then they *wanted* to try the third of the *3Rs—Reciprocation*—together.

## YOU + ME = US: THE NINE STEPS

These are the recommended steps in the *Reciprocation* stage that Carl and Suzanne followed.

---

### The Steps of Reciprocation

1. Explain to other people that there are fundamental differences between you and them.

   **You:**
2. (i) Describe to them how they see their world; and
   (ii) how and why this view causes them to behave the way they do.

**Me:**
3. Reveal to them how you see your world, and why and how your view affects your behavior.

**Us:**
4. Explore your differences—together.
5. Discover how your differences complement each other.
6. Examine how your differences can grate against each other in conflict.
7. Understand how your meanings become distorted in stress.
8. Appreciate the importance of tuning in on each other's Mood Frequency.
9. Reach mutual understanding.

---

Remember that before you begin the *Reciprocation* stage, both you and your partner must be in Acceptance.

As we have seen, unless you have met and satisfied your partner's needs, it is unlikely that they will be willing even to try to meet and satisfy yours. Therefore, you must have dealt with all their moods and satisfied their theme. They must be receptive.

You must also continue to stay tuned in on your partner's Mood Frequency so that you are speaking directly to who they are.

Carl and Suzanne, even though they had not been in contact with each other during the time they each went through the *Read* and *Respond* stages of the *3Rs,* now believed they were in Acceptance. Although slightly nervous, they were eager to try the *Reciprocation* Steps on each other. The first part of this technique—Steps 1 and 2—is described here. Steps 3 through 9 are covered in Chapters 11 and 12.

## STEP 1: EXPLAIN THE FUNDAMENTAL DIFFERENCES BETWEEN YOU AND THEM

Having shown that you understand your partner by meeting and satisfying their needs in *their* way, you should now explain that the way they think and feel about things is not the way *you* think and feel about them. That the ways each of you thinks about things are as different as fire and water.

Explain that this is not a value judgment—it is simply how things are.

You may want to suggest at this stage that how your partner looks at the world is so fundamental to who they are that it has influenced the way they have actually perceived, addressed, and been affected by the individual experiences of their lives.

The fact that they know you understand this may lead, in due course, to their trusting you enough to reveal those parts of themselves they may have kept hidden in secret anguish because they doubted *anyone* would ever understand and forgive them.

You should also explain to them that it is in fact those differences that have drawn the two of you together. That you *both* need those complementary differences to offset each other—to complete each other.

Carl and Suzanne, at this stage, understood the principles that defined each other's different personality types. They each tried to explain these differences to the other, using each other's Mood Frequency.

## YOU
### Step 2: Describe to Them How They See Their World

#### (i) Use their trigger as a starting point
Describe to the *Feelers* how they see things in terms of a world picture of what is "Fair/Unfair" (see page 141).

Tell them you know they are extremely sensitive to the delicate balance between what they perceive as just or unjust, equitable or inequitable, "fair or unfair" between people, and that they are emotionally offended by any tipping of this balance by the unfair use of any power (physical, intellectual, or emotional) intended to confuse, subordinate, or take advantage of another person. They want to right that unequal balance. And, being Feelers, they want to do it in as "soothing," non-controversial, and "fair" a way as possible.

In other words, they need to feel that *everyone* is being treated fairly.

Describe to the *Drivers* how they see things in terms of a world picture of what is "Right/Wrong," black/white.

Tell them you understand that, stemming from a very deepseated and rigid subjective "ethical code" of what is right and wrong, Drivers have an unbending and highly defined sense of the just, correct, and "honorable" way people should treat each other. This "ethical code" is what forms the basic identity of the Drivers: what they believe they are, and, in the best of all worlds, what all others should be.

Any behavior, reaction, idea, or opinion that falls outside the confines of this ethical code is taken as a personal affront. It is not deserving of their respect—is "wrong," almost "treasonable"—and must be shown to be so in no uncertain terms.

In other words, they need to know *everyone* is behaving in a certain predictably "right" way before they can respect them and feel at ease.

Describe to the *Analyzers* how they see things in terms of a world picture of what is "Rational/Irrational."

Tell them you understand that they have a sharply defined, reality-based standard of validity against which they measure people, ideas, and events. Those that measure up make coherent, rational sense and can be used productively. Those that don't quite measure up may be worked with, put into structured order, and organized so as to be made useful. Those that totally fail to measure up have no validity at all— are "irrational"—and can be dismissed out of hand.

In other words, that they want to hear everyone and everything making rational, logical sense.

Describe to the *Elitists* how they see things in terms of a world picture of what is "Appropriate/Inappropriate." Tell them you understand they represent a very rare class of people—like aristocrats, the very top echelon of society.

Tell them that whereas other personality types are only capable of seeing the world in terms of the things that affect them in the short term (by judging them as either "Fair/Unfair," "Right/Wrong," or "Rational/Irrational"), the Elitist sees his or her world from a wider, long-term, almost "visionary" perspective. Rather than limiting themselves to any one of the other personalities' considerations, Elitists move insightfully through all of them in an intellectually elegant way.

Elitists have a yardstick by which to measure people, ideas, and events. Since they invariably have the most insightful view, they have to measure everything by that standard: their own. They measure others in terms of whether or not they have a right to belong or participate in this vision, and therefore whether it is "Appropriate/Inappropriate" to include them in their view of the world.

Tell them you understand how depressing it can be for them when other people do not have the mental equipment to either match or understand their "vision." Tell them that because of this, it is often difficult for them to form close relationships, and they feel obliged to remain aloof and detached, relying on almost "scripted" charm to hold people off while still being polite.

Tell them you have gone to the trouble of finding out as much as you can about them because you admire who and what they are, and know how lonely it must be for them sometimes. Tell them you'd like to know more.

**(ii) Feed their own self-image back to them**

Follow through with illustrations of how and why they do and say things the way they do. (Use the *Self-Image* and *Mood Language* information in the relevant charts from pp. 142–49 and 154–55 as a guideline for your explanation.)

Emphasize that this is *their* way of doing things, and that even though you love it in them, you can't do it their way.

Remember you must tune in on their Mood Frequency when explaining it. For example, when Carl (the Analyzer) explained Suzanne (the Feeler) to herself:

**He Tuned In on Her *Feeler* Mood Frequency by:**

- Being low-key, toning down his own personality and concentrating on hers
- Lowering his voice and slowing down
- Being gentle, polite, empathetic, and genuine
- Speaking in terms of feelings
- Slowly and deliberately presenting one idea at a time
- Being sensitive to her physical reactions while he was speaking
- Not trying to dominate or control her, or "force" her to follow his line of thought
- Asking her directly what she thought/felt
- Patiently waiting while she sorted out her thoughts and feelings before replying. Not interrupting her or talking in her silences or pauses
- *Listening* to what she said—and understanding what she was saying *in her terms*

WHAT HE SAID:

"One of the things that makes me love you so much, Suzanne, is the way you're always so sensitive to my feelings. You've got an uncanny knack of knowing just when I'm even the slightest bit worried or upset about something.

HOW HE USED HER SELF-IMAGE TO EXPLAIN HER BEHAVIOR:

*Her Self-Image:*
—emotionally sensitive
*Her Mood Language:*
—aware of others' emotional states

"And I've noticed you always seem to be more aware of the feelings *behind* what I'm saying than what I'm actually saying.

—aware of the "feeling tone" of words
—thinks, speaks, and acts in terms of feelings

"I can see how—because you *are* so sensitive to that sort of thing—you are always so kind, gentle, and polite with everyone.

—behaves toward others in a warm, kind, gentle, and polite way

"I wish I were as sensitive as you are about that sort of thing, but I just don't seem capable of being that way.

"Am I right, here, in seeing you this way?"

Carl listened patiently to her reply. Then he presented another, separate idea:

"You always seem to be so fair and even-handed with everyone. You'll listen to everyone's opinion—no matter how crazy it sounds or how long it takes for them to get it out—before you make a decision.

*Her Self-Image:*
—fair and even-handed
*Her Mood Language:*
—considers everyone's point of view

"And you always appear to believe what they're saying!

—gives others the benefit of the doubt

"I wish I could be that patient—and that considerate—that *fair*. How do you manage it?"

Then the next idea:

"I love the way you're able to counterbalance my natural aggressiveness.

*Her Self-Image:*
—non-aggressive

"You never force your opinion on anyone the way I do. You're always so thoughtful and never pushy.

"Yet you always seem to be able to get everyone to agree on a fair and reasonable view in any situation. Remember that time I told our accountant straight out he didn't make sense and he took offense and was going to quit, and you came in and smoothed the waters?

"I think you're that way because you see everything in terms of what's fair or unfair. Am I right?"

*Her Mood Language:*
—does not try to dominate or control
—considers others' needs before her own
—is tactful and diplomatic
—acts as the peacemaker

When Suzanne (the Feeler) described Carl (the Analyzer) to himself she tuned in on his *Analyzer* Mood Frequency by:

- Concentrating her own ability to think clearly and logically
- Organizing and structuring her ideas and focusing on presenting them to him in logical sequence, as precisely and succinctly as possible
- Speaking in terms of facts (not opinions) that showed him in a positive light
- Remaining calm and controlled mentally and physically; never using emotional reasons to back up, justify, or demonstrate a fact
- Trying not to dominate or control him. Posing questions so that he could take control when he started explaining himself

**WHAT SHE SAID:**

**HOW SHE USED HIS SELF-IMAGE
TO EXPLAIN HIS BEHAVIOR:**

"What I love about you is the
way you always see things so
accurately: you're so rational
and clearsighted, sensible and
level-headed, direct and
straightforward about everything.

*His Self-Image:*
—sensible and level-headed; rational and clearsighted; direct
and straightforward

"Because you have this ability,
you never get sidetracked or go
off on tangents. And you never
get caught up in fuzzy thinking.

*His Mood Language:*
—considers everything irrational or emotional unimportant

"You simply see the facts. You
consider them in a way that
makes sense, and then you
make a decision based on
those facts.

—draws conclusions solely
from the facts, in a precise, ordered manner

"Whenever you come to a decision, it's always so obviously
logical and sensible. And when
you explain it to me in your
succinct way, I always wonder
why I never saw it that way
before.

—moves unerringly and systematically to his "bottom line"
—speaks directly and assert-
ively

"You have this uncanny ability
of being able to weigh what's
useful and what isn't, then taking what's useful and making it
work to our advantage.

—reacts in terms of what is for
and against him personally

"I wish I could do that. It's so
much more sensible and productive than the way I see
things. But, hard as I try, I
can't. Tell me how you do it."

Follow these guidelines in describing your partner to him-
or herself, adjusting the style and manner to suit the personality of the person you are addressing.

You will be pleasantly surprised at your partner's reaction.
He or she will be amazed that anyone—and especially you,

the person they care for most—can understand them so deeply, so sympathetically, so well.

---

### "The Right Chemistry"

The passionate, romantic love of heart-thumping, sweaty-palmed euphoria, which is triggered by mutual initial attraction, is accompanied by a flooding of the brain with amphetamine-like chemicals such as dopamine, norepinephrine, and phenylethylamine.

We are so elated by this natural high, we actually feel we are floating or walking on air, and the silly looks on our faces broadcast our delirium to the world.

However, after about two to three years of being smitten, our bodies build up a tolerance to these effervescent chemicals, and the "buzz" begins to lose its intensity.

At this stage, relationships can fizzle out and die.

If, however, we start to respond to the object of our love, rather than merely to our own joy at being in love, the self-involving passion of early love is overtaken by the more considerate compassion of mature love.

We begin to cherish our lovers for who *they* are, rather than for how they make *us* feel. With this development, other chemicals set to work in our brains. These are endorphins: soothing chemicals, akin to natural painkillers, that give us the calming sense of security we feel in our love, and in our lover.

Unlike the chemicals that come into play with our initial attraction, the chemicals behind our joy of attachment and togetherness do not fade with time.

As long as our Mutual Acceptance and understanding keep developing and strengthening, the endorphins in our brains continue to provide us with a "narcotic" sense of comfort, completeness, and well-being.

ELEVEN

# How to Get Others to Understand Who You Are

Having explained to the persons whose love and understanding is important to you that there are fundamental differences between you and them, and having demonstrated that you understand how they see their world, you are now ready to move on to the third step in *Reciprocation,* when you explain who you are.

## ME
### STEP 3: REVEAL TO THEM HOW YOU SEE YOUR WORLD, AND WHY AND HOW YOUR VIEW AFFECTS YOUR BEHAVIOR

By this stage, you understand yourself—why you do and say things the way you do—and should have no trouble explaining yourself to the persons you want to understand you.

However, we suggest you go about it in the following order:

**Use your own trigger as a starting point**
Keeping tuned in on their Mood Frequency, explain how different your own is from theirs.

188

For example, Carl revealed how his trigger works to Suzanne this way:

> Much as I love the way you see things in terms of what is "Fair" or "Unfair," *I* don't—and can't—see things in those terms.
>
> I see things in terms of what is "Rational" or "Irrational"—it's just the way my brain is set up. Just as you can't change the way you feel about things, I can't alter the way I think about the same things. You think with your heart, I think with my head. Maybe that's why I need you so much; you make up for what I lack. I need your softness and gentleness as much as you need my precision and astuteness.

### Explain your own personality in terms of your own Mood Language

In other words, start with your own behavior and the way you do and say things, and relate it back to the way you view things as either "Fair/Unfair," "Right/Wrong," "Rational/Irrational," or "Appropriate/Inappropriate."

Carl explained himself like this:

> I think, act, and speak clearly, succinctly, and analytically. I need to draw conclusions solely from the facts, in a precise, ordered manner—so that I can make "rational," logical sense of things.
>
> To my mind, emotions and feelings get in the way of my ability to do this, so I have to push them into the background . . . control them. Unlike you, I don't have the innate ability to read people's feelings and make sense out of them, so I have to concentrate on what they're saying and the way they're saying it.
>
> I need to consider everything seriously and earnestly,

so I get impatient when people—to my way of thinking—behave facetiously or glibly or shallowly.

I know I tend to say exactly what I mean without proper regard for others' feelings, but to my mind that is the way I see things.

I can see how you with your sensitivity to feelings think I am being insensitive. But just as you have to evaluate the world through feelings, I have to evaluate it through reason.

So, just as you really have no choice in reacting to things the way you do, neither do I.

Can you get a feel for the different way I think about everything?"

## US
### Step 4: Explore Your Differences—Together

Now that you both understand each other's very different way of viewing the world, it should be time to discover—together—what it is about each other that you need, and why.

Examine those apparently opposing ways you each have of thinking and feeling, of saying and doing things, and notice how neatly they counterbalance and complement each other. One of you supplies only half of your shared completeness. The other supplies the other half.

Take your time discussing, and appreciating, those differences that each of you relies on to become "complete."

### Step 5: Discover How Your Differences Complement Each Other

This is where you rediscover what it was that instinctively drew you to each other originally. You need, first, to identify those particular differences about each other that you love,

respect, and admire; and second, to realize how those differences complement each other.

*Remember: Stay in Acceptance of each other.* Accept what
the other person means and not what you think he or she
means, (in other words, trust them). Focus only on the positive features of each other's personality. *Do not,* at this stage,
discuss how your differences grate.

## "Basically What I Like About You Is the Fact That You Like Me"

To get the optimum result from this process of rediscovery:
First, you should identify one of the strongest traits that you
admire in this person you care for, and tell him or her what
it is so he or she know you appreciate it. For example, a
*Feeler* could tell a *Driver:* "One thing I really like a lot about
you is the way you make friends for us so easily at first meeting. You seem to draw people with your enthusiastic interest
in them. Then you keep everyone riveted with your great stories and sense of humor—I find that very impressive."

Second, the other person should identify the counterbalancing trait in you. For example, the *Driver* would tell the
*Feeler:* "Well, I'm impressed by the way you keep our friends
for us in the long term. You always keep up with them, remember what's important to them, always ask after their kids
. . . You're so considerate of everybody."

Finally, you should discover together how each of you
needs that other person's way of doing and saying things to
balance your own. For example, the *Feeler* would suggest: "I
guess without your instant impact we wouldn't *have* any
friends, because I just don't have that spontaneous outgoing
charm you do. It just isn't me."

And the *Driver* could counter: "Sure, but without your genuine, warm interest in them, we wouldn't *keep* them. I lose
interest in them once I know all about them. But that's exactly when you're at your best." And conclude:

"So between us we seem to cover all the bases as far as making and keeping friends are concerned. Not a bad team!"

## "He Needs Me the Way I Am as Much as I Need Him the Way He Is"

At this stage of the *Reciprocation* process, a young couple who agreed to test and use the *3Rs* suddenly understood the roots of their mutual attraction, and their counterbalancing need of each other.

Nicole is a *Driver*, with an infectious exuberance, a wonderfully expressive face, and a wickedly sharp sense of humor, who is perceptive and aware of everything that is happening around her. She sums people up almost instantaneously, and instinctively knows how to put them at ease and thoroughly charm them—if she cares to.

Sam is a *Feeler*, whose disarmingly warm, sensitive approach to people, gentle sense of humor, and insatiable curiosity about the world make his gregarious nature even more appealing. He is slow to judge people, always seeing the best in everyone.

Nicole is twenty-three and Sam twenty-eight. They had both been deeply wounded in previous relationships, and even though they had been lovers for two years, each was still tentative about *completely* trusting the other, and subconsciously held back from sharing themselves totally.

As they explored their differences, they discovered just how snugly the variously shaped pieces of each other's personalities fitted together into a harmonized whole.

When they understood the deep need each of them had (equally) to be counterbalanced and complemented by the other, their lingering doubts about trust disappeared in a new sense of transferred confidence and security in the other person. Each of them discovered: He/She needs the way I am *as much as* I need the way he/she is. He/She actually *likes* me the way I am!

He loved her quick decisiveness—the way she managed immediately to home in on the essentials of anything, decide exactly what they meant, make an almost instantaneous judgment, and form a very definite opinion.

She loved his thoughtful open-mindedness—the way he managed to consider everything thoroughly and patiently, mull over all the possible interpretations, and proffer the fairest solution in good time.

They realized that—combining these two very different ways of reacting to the world, treating each other's views with respect—they each gained new and valuable insights into things that, alone, they would have been unaware of. They also realized that at those times when a quick decision was needed, he relied on, and trusted, her to make it; whereas at those times when a more in-depth decision was required, she just as trustingly relied on him to supply it.

He loved her strong and definite opinions about everything. He loved the way she would react indignantly to things she thought were not "right" in that exciting, dramatic way she had, and he loved it when she made pithy comments with her wickedly irreverent sense of humor.

She loved his considered and deeply thought out opinions about things. She loved the way he reacted unhurriedly and would never think of hurting anyone's feelings—even when they weren't within earshot. She loved his gentle sense of humor.

They discovered that they both felt somehow comforted and made secure by each other's approval of their own reactions. She felt that if he didn't consider her behavior "over the top," actually enjoyed her dramatic reactions, and regarded her opinions with respect as being worthwhile, then she was validated in being who she was. She didn't have to pretend to be anyone else. He liked her the way she was.

He felt that since she didn't consider him indecisive, actually respected the way he'd only make a decision after he'd considered everything, took his opinions very seriously, and enjoyed his humor, she confirmed and sanctioned who he was.

They both realized they could "be themselves" because the other person actually liked the way they were.

He admired her ability to face any issue head-on and say di-

She respected his "laid-back" ability to let things take their

rectly what she thought about it without any extraneous considerations of "fear or favor." own course without his interference.

They discovered that he moderated her frequently mercurial, on-the-spot judgments, and she stimulated his frequently overaccommodating lack of reaction.

They also realized that their differences gave each of them a mutually trustworthy standard against which they could gauge their own reactions. She realized she trusted his respect for her so much that if he indicated he thought she had gone too far, she probably had; and he found that if she let him know that he should finally "do something," he trusted her judgment so thoroughly that he felt bound to step in.

She loved his protective gentleness, his reliable deliberation, and his consideration for her feelings even at the expense of his own.
She liked the way everyone liked him.

He loved her passionate assuredness, spontaneous unpredictability, and fierce loyalty to him.
He liked the way other people admired her.

In fact, they liked almost everything about each other. They each loved how the other made them feel needed and important. They both felt not only loved but loving.

## STEP 6: EXAMINE HOW YOUR DIFFERENCES CAN GRATE AGAINST EACH OTHER IN CONFLICT

This is the stage where you both come to an understanding of how your differences can rub each other the wrong way with the onset of stress and rejection.

However, you should *not* move into this stage until you have both fully realized just how much you admire and need each other's particular way of reacting to the world and each other.

**(i)** Having explained each of your triggers in Steps 2 and 3, you should now discuss how everybody has a trigger that can be set off and send them into rejection. Discuss how, in feeling rejected, we all reject the person who is rejecting us.

With mutual rejection our filters slip, exposing our Dominant Moods, which are now firmly in place as self-protective shields against attack. Our Dominant Moods also arm us with all our old familiar self-serving, manipulative tactics for either fighting or fleeing the person who is rejecting us.

The greater the stress of rejection, the further we retreat into our core personality, and draw on all the other Moods of Rejection to protect ourselves and get the other person to agree with us.

When you discuss this aspect of rejection, keep it universal, general, and objective. Discuss it in terms of how *everybody* is affected this way.

**(ii)** Once you can both comfortably acknowledge that this is what happens to everyone in rejection, turn to an examination of your own triggers and your respective Dominant Moods that become your personal shield against attack.

Be cautious at this stage. Stay in Acceptance and examine each other objectively. Do not allow blame or reproach to shift you into the Moods of Rejection. If you can do this with a sense of humor, all the better—learn to laugh at yourselves.

Begin with each of the traits you find appealing in each other when you are in Mutual Acceptance. Then carefully examine how each of these same traits can *suddenly appear to change character* when they are intensified and directed against each other in the stress of rejection—turning into apparently threatening and hostile traits.

### The Flip Side

Sam began with Nicole's Driver trait of passionate enthusiasm that he found so appealing when she was in Acceptance of him. He then carefully examined how, in rejection, this very same trait intensified into the all-out, overwhelming, and dramatic Mood of Anger she directed at him. In other words, he saw that she was as passionately enthusiastic in her rejection of him as she was in her Acceptance of him.

All of the traits that he disliked so much in her when they argued were not incomprehensible perversions of who she was, but merely extensions of the very same traits he admired in her. Her character did not change in conflict—it was his *perception* of her character that changed.

Nicole began with Sam's Feeler trait of emotional sensitivity and saw how, in rejection, it intensified into the hypersensitive "touchiness" he displayed over anything she said or did to him.

In reexamining the birthday party incident, Carl noted this same intensification of Suzanne's emotional sensitivity when she was in rejection. He finally saw how and why she "overreacted" emotionally. The same quality he loved in her in Acceptance had become the very quality he had not been able to understand or deal with when she was in rejection.

However, now he realized that—given who she was—she could no more change this aspect of her character than he could change any aspect of his. But he could *understand* it: it suddenly made sense. He no longer saw her reaction as merely an irrational piece of nonsense, but as a necessary and valid part of the integrity of her personality.

And Suzanne, in examining Carl's Analyzer trait of rational directness, realized for the first time that when he had compared the gifts at his birthday party, he had not in fact been rejecting *her*. He had merely been acting in accordance with the integrity of *his* personality. There had been no malicious intention to embarrass her or make her look foolish at all. She had misread his motives.

Suzanne now saw how Carl's traits that she loved so much in him when they were in Acceptance of each other became the very things about him she misunderstood and misinterpreted when she was in rejection of him.

What had caused her to misinterpret his action, and what

had caused him to misunderstand her reaction to it, was the fact that, in rejection, we all see each other myopically through our own Dominant Mood—*we judge others solely in our own terms.*

In other words, when we are in rejection, we cease entirely being open-minded and objective, and instead become blinkered, narrow-minded, and entirely subjective.

Simply by *understanding* what happens to each other in rejection, we find we can no longer automatically assume that each other's intentions are completely mean-spirited, ill-conceived, and base.

The following "Clash" Charts illustrate how the four personality types actually perceive one another's behavior in mutual rejection. It shows how each type's Dominant Mood gives a false coloring to his or her perception of what the other person is *really* doing and saying.

Use these charts as a guideline in your exploration of how your personality traits can grate against each other when your Dominant Moods of Rejection clash head-on.

### HOW THE FEELER AND THE DRIVER CLASH IN MUTUAL REJECTION

**How the FEELER sees the Driver**

*Trigger:* "Unfair"
*Dominant Mood:* Bargaining

*How the Driver's traits (which were accepted in Indignation) are seen now they are intensified in Anger:*

Driver's *passionate enthusiasm* is now seen as inexcusably extreme, out of control, over the top Anger
Driver's Anger is seen as rudeness, and a barrier against the Feeler's bonding attempts. Feeler is confused, stunned,

**How the DRIVER sees the Feeler**

*Trigger:* "Wrong"
*Dominant Mood:* Anger

*How the Feeler's traits (which were accepted in Conciliation) are seen now they are intensified in Bargaining:*

Feeler's *fairness and even-handedness* are now seen as lack of loyalty to the Driver. Consideration for everyone and his/her dog's point of view are seen as failure to hold a strong opinion on anything.
Feeler's *emotional sensitivity*

hurt, and overwhelmed, and re-coils from Driver's bluntness, harshness, crassness, and earthy comments, which are seen as forms of "unfair" ag-gression

Driver's constant interrup-tions, talking over, repetitions, and not listening are seen as a closed-minded inability to con-sider anyone's point of view but his/her own

Driver's *assertion and direct-ness* are now seen as tyrannical attempts to control, dominate, and victimize

Driver seen as a "control freak," who will not rest easy until he/she has browbeaten the Feeler into doing things his/her way

Driver's insistence on having the last word and coming out on top is seen as unfair bul-lying

Driver's *perceptiveness and quick thinking* are now seen as unfair ways to manipulate and play games with the Feeler's emotions, attacking everything faster than he/she can follow. The Feeler feels he/she is never being given a chance to breathe, but is being over-whelmed and smothered

*From the Feeler's Bargaining point of view:* The Driver's Anger allows for no give-and-take—there is no way to bargain with Anger. Being non-confrontational, he/she is un-able to counter Anger and feels intimidated and victimized in the face of an unfair onslaught

is now seen as a form of emo-tional manipulation, and over-emotional reactions and dis-plays are seen as false and hyp-ocritical. Driver cannot under-stand why Feeler stays locked in on some petty, irrelevant, emotional point, and sees this as a weakness of character

Feeler's *non-aggressiveness* is now seen as lack of interest in the Driver.

Feeler's unwillingness to con-front him/her is seen as a way of ignoring the Driver. The more he/she tries, unsuccess-fully, to get a rise out of the Feeler, the more of a bully he/she is made to feel.

Feeler's tendency to close down and turn inward is seen as indifference

Feeler's *slower, considered re-actions* are seen as attempts to purposely frustrate and infuri-ate the Driver

Feeler's inability to keep up—to follow what is being said and to give quick re-sponses—is viewed as slow-witted stupidity

*From the Driver's Anger point of view:* The Feeler's Bar-gaining does not allow for head-on confrontation—there is no way to bring everything out into the open, face it directly, and deal with it. The Driver is unable to get a rise out of Bar-gaining and feels frustrated and dismissed

In mutual rejection,
the Feeler and the Driver
are each other's *nemesis*

## HOW THE FEELER AND THE ANALYZER CLASH IN MUTUAL REJECTION

### How the FEELER sees the Analyzer

*Trigger:* "Unfair"
*Dominant Mood:* Bargaining

*How the Analyzer's traits (which were accepted in Dismissal) are seen now they are intensified in Denial:*

Analyzer's *rationality and clearsightedness* now seen as cold, impersonal fixation on the least important aspect of any conflict

Analyzer's lack of any emotional display and apparent lack of awareness of the emotional impact of the conflict bothers the Feeler deeply

Analyzer's *sense and levelheadedness* now seen as being totally devoid of feeling, emotionally bankrupt

Analyzer's focus on purely factual reasoning, without consideration of emotional factors, is seen as cold and inhuman

Analyzer's *directness and straightforwardness* now seen as downright rudeness and a rough rejection of any Bargaining offers. It is taken as a personal insult

Analyzer's attempts to blandly control and dominate are deeply resented

### How the ANALYZER sees the Feeler

*Trigger:* "Irrational"
*Dominant Mood:* Denial

*How the Feeler's traits (which were accepted in Conciliation) are seen now they are intensified in Bargaining:*

Feeler's *fairness and evenhandedness* now seen as willingness to cooperate with the Analyzer intellectually, and to be led

Feeler's willingness to bend, concede, and back down is seen as a weakness in intellectual integrity that can be taken advantage of

Feeler's *emotional sensitivity* now viewed as irrelevant to the issue and out of place. It is seen as an undisciplined lack of control

Analyzer sees Feeler as allowing emotional clouding to interfere with his/her logical thought and focus, and perceives this as a way to adopt the role of superior

Feeler's *non-aggression* seen as lack of strongly held position and lack of intellectual strength

Feeler's compliance is seen as willingness to accept control and dominance of Analyzer's will

*From the Feeler's Bargaining point of view:* The Analyzer's Denial is viewed as flat, blunt Anger and is rejected. It allows for no give-and-take, and there is no emotion to bond with

*From the Analyzer's Denial point of view:* The Feeler's Bargaining is seen as intellectual weakness and permission to be manipulated

### HOW THE FEELER AND THE ELITIST CLASH IN MUTUAL REJECTION

**How the FEELER sees the Elitist**

*Trigger:* "Unfair"
*Dominant Mood:* Bargaining

*How the Elitist's traits (which were accepted in Exclusiveness) are seen now they are intensified in Depression:*

Elitist's *intellectual power* is now seen as being used to take unfair advantage in dominating and controlling the Feeler
Elitist's intellectual reasoning is seen as lacking in emotional sensitivity

Elitist's *superior attitude* is now seen as an unwillingness to bond and a rejection of the Feeler's empathetic approach
Elitist's withdrawal and aloofness now seen as withdrawal and an unwillingness to share feelings
Elitist's assumption of superiority is seen as rudeness, and is considered unfounded and ill-earned

Elitist's *depth and complexity* are now perceived by the Feeler as his/her own fault in not being able to empathize with the Elitist

**How the ELITIST sees the Feeler**

*Trigger:* "Inappropriate"
*Dominant Mood:* Depression

*How the Feeler's traits (which were accepted in Conciliation) are seen now they are intensified in Bargaining:*

Feeler's *fairness and even-handedness* are seen as a lack of strength of ego, a lack of intellectual integrity and purpose, and viewed as weakness
Feeler's insistence on considering all points of view and failing to focus solely on Elitist's needs are seen as disloyalty

Feeler's *emotional sensitivity* is seen as misdirected, poorly thought out, and inappropriate
Feeler's overemphasis on emotionality at the expense of reason is seen as an inability to comprehend the full context of anything. The Elitist considers the Feeler an unworthy opponent

Feeler's *non-aggressiveness* is seen as cowardly caution
Feeler's non-confrontational attitude is seen as lacking the heart to take risks, and the Elit-

ist has no respect for anyone who backs away from his/her own aggression

*From the Feeler's Bargaining point of view:* The Elitist's Depression is viewed as a form of Anger, which causes closure against the Feeler, leaving him/her nothing to bargain or bond with

*From the Elitist's Depression point of view:* The Feeler's Bargaining is seen as a pathetic attempt to sidestep the main issue emotionally

### HOW THE DRIVER AND THE ANALYZER CLASH IN MUTUAL REJECTION

**How the DRIVER sees the Analyzer**

*Trigger:* "Wrong"
*Dominant Mood:* Anger

*How the Analyzer's traits (which were accepted in Dismissal) are seen now they are intensified in Denial:*

Analyzer's *rationality and clearsightedness* are now seen as giving a superficial, narrow-visioned view of only one aspect of the situation
Analyzer is seen as having a one-track mind and being incapable of grasping the bigger issue

Analyzer's *sense and levelheadedness* are now seen as lacking in involving passion, human sensitivity, and verve
Analyzer is seen as being too detached from, and unaffected by, the emotional excitement of conflict, and the Driver views this as being one-dimensional

Analyzer's *directness and straightforwardness* are now

**How the ANALYZER sees the Driver**

*Trigger:* "Irrational"
*Dominant Mood:* Denial

*How the Driver's traits (which were accepted in Indignation) are seen now they are intensified in Anger:*

Driver's *assertion and directness* now seen as the Driver's being too opinionated. Driver is seen as relying on extravagant opinions rather than rationally ordered and considered facts
Driver's assertions now taken as personal criticism, which have to be denied, and attempts to control and dominate are rejected

Driver's *passionate enthusiasm* now seen as showing a lack of control and focus
Driver's dramatic, theatrical behavior is seen as emotionally off-balance, totally out of place, and not deserving of respect

Driver's *quick thinking and perception* now seen as uncon-

seen as an inability to draw on anything but rational facts to substantiate his/her side of any conflict. Analyzer's inability to draw on everything to orchestrate and manipulate an argument is seen as a failing that can be used against him/her

Analyzer's attempts to control and dominate through force of pure reason are seen as inadequate, and disappoint the Driver, who thought he/she might have found a worthy opponent

*From the Driver's Anger point of view:* The Analyzer's Denial is what causes an entrenched and narrow, one-dimensional approach

trolled, undisciplined, disorganized thinking.

Driver's "opinions" are rejected—only "facts" are acceptable. Even the facts the Driver throws are denied, as there are too many of them, and they are jumbled.

Driver's jumping from subject to subject is seen as a failure to stay on track and focused, and is irritating and frustrating to the Analyzer

*From the Analyzer's Denial point of view:* The Driver's Anger is what causes lack of focus

### How the Driver and the Elitist Clash in Mutual Rejection

**How the DRIVER sees the Elitist**

*Trigger:* "Wrong"
*Dominant Mood:* Anger

*How the Elitist's traits (which were accepted in Exclusiveness) are seen now they are intensified in Depression:*

Elitist's *superior attitude* is now seen as an unwillingness to enter wholeheartedly into the drama of conflict

Elitist's condescension is seen as a way of avoiding having to keep up with the Driver and participate in his/her word games

Elitist's *intellectual power* is now seen as giving greater mental discipline and control over the Driver

**How the ELITIST sees the Driver**

*Trigger:* "Inappropriate"
*Dominant Mood:* Depression

*How the Driver's traits (which were accepted in Indignation) are seen now they are intensified in Anger:*

Driver's *passionate enthusiasm* is now seen as a way of melodramatically presenting only the Driver's own side of any argument

Driver is seen as a self-promoting exhibitionist

Driver's *quick thinking and perception* now seen as a lack of control over intellectual direction and focus. Driver is

Elitist's intellectually patronizing manner irritates the Driver, who then tries to outsmart to show that the Elitist is in no position to be patronizing

Elitist's *depth and complexity* are now seen as an inability to work out what the Elitist wants, an inability to communicate his/her quandary, and an inability to ask advice

*From the Driver's Anger point of view:* The Elitist's Depression (like Bargaining) is seen as an attempt to hold the Driver off and close him/her out. The Driver thinks it is something he/she said or did in Anger that caused the Elitist's Depression

seen as a smart aleck who enjoys playing games, and his/her quick changes of direction confuse and irritate the Elitist

However, Driver's "must-win" attitude is admired and respected by the Elitist, but causes clash over who the real winner will be

Driver's *assertion and directness* now seen as undignified rudeness and an inappropriate attempt to control and dominate

*From the Elitist's Depression point of view:* The Driver's Anger is seen as an attempt to manipulate and play with his/her thoughts and feelings

## HOW THE ANALYZER AND THE ELITIST CLASH IN MUTUAL REJECTION

**How the ANALYZER sees the Elitist**

*Trigger:* "Irrational"
*Dominant Mood:* Denial

*How the Elitist's traits (which were accepted in Exclusiveness) are seen now they are intensified in Depression:*

Elitist's *intellectual power* is now seen as an effort to control and dominate

Elitist's presentation of information is seen as being too convoluted, too long-winded, and straying from the point

Elitist's opinions and emotional displays, unless backed up by facts, are rejected

**How the ELITIST sees the Analyzer**

*Trigger:* "Inappropriate"
*Dominant Mood:* Depression

*How the Analyzer's traits (which were accepted in Dismissal) are seen now they are intensified in Denial:*

Analyzer's *rationality and clearsightedness* now seen as narrow-visioned failure to address the whole problem

Analyzer's insistence on focusing solely on the logical "facts" of any issue is seen as failure to grasp the full range of causal factors involved

Elitist's *superior attitude* is now seen as a way of forcing the Analyzer to accept his/her opinion as correct and the only possible way of looking at the problem. It is seen as personal criticism

Elitist's condescension is seen as suggesting that there are secrets about logic, emotions, and life the Analyzer would just not understand

Elitist's *depth and complexity* are now seen as merely a lack of focus and clarity in thinking. Elitist's display of emotional affect is seen as hypocritical and manipulative

Elitist's mixture of facts, personal opinions, and emotionality is seen as a way of passing judgment on the Analyzer

*From the Analyzer's Denial point of view:* The Elitist's Depression is caused by miscalculation of thought and logic. If only he/she would listen to the Analyzer's reason, he/she would be free of melancholy

Analyzer's *directness and straightforwardness* now seen as rudeness, a lack of tact and sensitivity, and an inability to empathize with what the Elitist is going through

Analyzer's blunt comments seen as highly critical personal attacks and a challenge to the Elitist's superiority

Analyzer's *sense and level-headedness* now seen as superficial and lacking in depth of understanding

Analyzer's pragmatism is seen as intentional disregard for the Elitist's expressed emotional needs. Analyzer's soberness and lack of humor become an irritating dullness

*From the Elitist's Depression point of view:* The Analyzer's Denial is now seen as a perverse inability to see the emotional depth and impact of the problem that gives the Elitist nothing to reach out to for empathetic understanding

In mutual rejection,
the Analyzer and the Elitist
are each other's *nemesis*

The preceding charts show how people of different personality types see each other when they are in mutual rejection: they see each other as being very different from themselves.

Amazingly, so do people of the same type. In rejection, they recognize all the "good features" of their own personality type in others of the same type not at all. Rather, in mutual rejection, people of the same type see each other in the following ways:

*Feelers in mutual rejection* see other Feelers as being weak, indecisive, overemotional, and unable to commit or follow through on what they believe.

They see them as allowing themselves to become victims, and "unfairly" and pathetically asking to be treated more gently and protectively because of their victim status.

In mutual rejection, Feelers see other Feelers as "wimps."

*Drivers in mutual rejection* see other Drivers as being slightly off-balance mentally and emotionally, being completely overwhelming, too disorganized, and too bossy and controlling.

They believe they are simply "wrong" in what they're saying, and "off the wall" in the way they're saying it.

In mutual rejection, Drivers see other Drivers as simply "crazy."

*Analyzers in mutual rejection* see other Analyzers as being inefficient, focused on the wrong things, too assertive and dogmatic, and overly sensitive to imagined personal attacks.

They see them as behaving "irrationally," in an unself-disciplined and unacceptable way.

In mutual rejection, Analyzers see other Analyzers as an unorganized "mess."

*Elitists in mutual rejection* see other Elitists as intellectually sloppy, overly sentimental, self-centered poseurs who thrive on self-pity.

They see them as being "inappropriately" and unwarrantedly pretentious.

In mutual rejection, Elitists see other Elitists as nothing more than "all gas and gaiters."

# TWELVE

# How We Distort
# Each Other's Meaning

By this stage, you and the person whose understanding is so important to you have explored your personality type differences. You have discovered how those differences, which complement each other so well when you are getting along together, become the very things that grate against each other when you are in conflict.

You should now move on to the next step in *Reciprocation* when—together—you and your partner come to understand that what each of you may actually say in these conflicts is *not* what the other one really hears.

## STEP 7: UNDERSTAND HOW YOUR MEANINGS BECOME DISTORTED IN STRESS

Having understood how, in mutual rejection, each of you sees the other's behavior solely and exclusively through the lens of your own Dominant Mood and interprets it narrowly *in your own terms only,* you should now explore how that

Dominant Mood also controls what each of you *actually* sees and hears.

When, at his birthday party, Carl held up Suzanne's gift in one hand and the friend's present in his other and said to her, "Now this is a *real* gift! Why can't you give me something like this?" that is *not* what she "heard" him say. As she took in his words and watched what he was doing, only certain fragments of their meaning were absorbed—the rest bounced off the protective shield of her Dominant Mood. Her Dominant Mood distorted his *meaning.*

Again, this was not done perversely, maliciously, or on purpose. In rejection, everyone's Dominant Mood causes a distortion of meaning, because only certain portions of that meaning get through, and even those portions that are absorbed undergo a distortion.

As we have seen, a person's meaning is communicated through a combination of verbal (voice) and non-verbal (body) language. While we all rely chiefly on words to disclose the rational meaning we intend to convey, the way we use those words and the way our body reacts as we deliver those words imparts a more complete story. The complete story involves how we think *and* feel about what we are actually saying. Our full meaning has both a rational *and* an emotional content.

Intentionally or unintentionally, consciously or subconsciously, both our voice and our body are communicating what we are *thinking* rationally and cognitively and what we are *feeling* emotionally. Our meaning conveys both thoughts and feelings.

Normally, when we are in Acceptance, we are capable of reading the real meaning of another person's communicated thoughts and feelings pretty much as they intend us to understand them.

However, in rejection, each of us becomes incapable of

reading other people's real meaning clearly. In our own particular way, each of us distorts their meaning so that the message we receive is *not* what they intended us to understand at all.

### "But I Didn't Mean That!": What Happens in Rejection

In *Rejection,* as people withdraw into their core personality, their Dominant Mood acts as an almost impenetrable self-protective shield. Just about everything you say to them will be deflected off this shield (through the use of the Moods of Rejection: Anger, Depression, Bargaining, and Denial).

Nothing you say or do is viewed objectively: everything is interpreted subjectively *in their terms.* Only certain fragments of what you are saying manage to penetrate, and even these become greatly distorted by their Dominant Mood.

### "I Think I Know What You Mean":
### What Happens in Acceptance

In *Acceptance,* as there is no threat and therefore no need to fight or flee, people allow their filter to "soften" their Dominant Mood, rendering it more receptive. Because their filter is making their Dominant Mood more tolerantly accessible, much more of what you are saying can actually penetrate the shield, suffering only slight distortion. They are more receptive to your real meaning.

However, even in Acceptance, that part of your meaning which does get through to them is still slightly distorted. Their filter has already put its own spin on your meaning and reinterpreted it in their terms.

The spin that each personality type puts on your meaning depends on their general view of the world and their particular view of you and your behavior.

The following section explains the particular spin different personality types put on the meaning of what they see and

hear, subtly changing its meaning *even when they are in Acceptance;* and how they deflect almost everything they see
and hear *when they are in rejection.*

Remember this is not done perversely, maliciously, or with
the intention of alienating you—it is merely part of who they
are.

| | | |
|---|---|---|
| THE FEELER | *Dominant Mood:* | Bargaining |
| | *Filter:* | Conciliation |
| | *Trigger:* | "Fair/Unfair" |

Provided you satisfy the Feelers' Conciliation belief that
you are being fair and even-handed, trying to bond, willing
to trust, and continue to speak to them in terms of feelings,
they will understand your meaning as clearly as is possible
for them.

However, if you set off their "Unfair" trigger and send them
into rejection, the *only* thing that gets through to them is *their
interpretation of the emotional intention behind your words
and actions.* Only their feeling receptors are on sharp alert—
nothing else gets through! Specific words and specific actions
have no meaning apart from the emotional impact they deliver.

For example, if Nicole yells at Sam: "You're a low-down,
mean, thoughtless S.O.B!" what he hears would be "I hate
you!" Two seconds after she yelled at him, he would probably
be unable to remember the specific words she used. All he
can remember is the emotional impact of her verbal and
physical behavior—that is all that got through to him.

When Carl said, "Now this is a *real* gift! Why can't you give
me something like this?" Suzanne heard something like: "I
don't like you, I don't like your gift, I prefer my friends to
you!" When she was asked to repeat Carl's specific words—
which she had to be reminded of—she put her own interpretation on them. That was what she *actually heard* him say.

Everything else was deflected off the shield of her Dominant Mood.

| | | |
|---|---|---|
| **THE DRIVER** | *Dominant Mood:* | Anger |
| | *Filter:* | Indignation |
| | *Trigger:* | "Right/Wrong" |

In Acceptance, the Driver sees and hears just about everything that interests him. Provided you do not arouse his Indignation too much by being too boring, too stupid, or too nebulous, he objectively picks up everything directed at him (and around him), and rapidly extracts and concentrates on those essential features that interest him.

However, once you trigger his "Wrong" switch and send him into rejection, all his sensory receptors switch to full alert and begin to concentrate on a very narrow band. He sees and hears exactly what you're saying and doing *in the real world,* but judges it solely in his terms of what you are doing and saying "wrong." Nothing escapes him, but since it is coming at him in extremely sharp "wrong" focus, everything you say and do is fuel for his Anger—and he will attack and manipulate it.

As every nuance of your verbal and physical behavior is being absorbed and interpreted at rapid-fire speed, he is already ten seconds ahead of you and impatiently leaps backward and forward through the argument, collecting ammunition for a shotgun attack.

For example, if Sam yells at Nicole: "You're a mean, conniving, thoughtless cow!" she would hear every single word he says, see every minute expression on his face, and the slightest movement of his body. Although she misses none of his reasoning and emotional meaning, she interprets it solely in terms of what he is saying and doing "wrong." Before he has even had time to draw breath, she will probably be extravagantly attacking anything and everything he is, has been, or will be thinking and feeling about their argument.

THE ANALYZER   *Dominant Mood:*  Denial
                 *Filter:*  Dismissal
                 *Trigger:*  "Rational/Irrational"

In Acceptance, the Analyzer sees and hears those things that make sense and can be used to best advantage. She simply dismisses, without showing any interest in them whatsoever, those things that to her mind do not make rational sense.

However, once you set off her "Irrational" trigger and send her into rejection, her Denial shield falls firmly into place. Only those words that make rational sense and mean something that can be analyzed and weighed penetrate; everything else simply bounces off the shield. She disciplines and controls herself to hear only verbal, rational, sequentially delivered, concrete facts. She denies the impact of anything that is not presented to her in this way.

Suzanne's reaction to Carl's words set off his "Irrational" trigger and threw him into rejection. In rejection, he denied the fact that his words could possibly have had an adverse effect on her. Suzanne's emotional reaction simply bounced off his Denial shield. It made no rational sense, so it did not penetrate.

THE ELITIST   *Dominant Mood:*  Depression
              *Filter:*  Exclusiveness
              *Trigger:*  "Appropriate/
                        Inappropriate"

In Acceptance, the Elitist stands back from, but still takes in, everything that is said and done. He only allows those things that he considers "appropriate" to touch and affect him personally. Provided you act and react to him within his "appropriate" bounds, what you say and do is absorbed through his Exclusiveness filter and is acceptable to him.

However, once his "Inappropriate" trigger has been tripped and he moves into rejection, he may withdraw behind the Dominant Mood shield of either the Feeler, the Driver, or the Analyzer. He will then move from one shield to another depending on the response he gets. In his failure to receive the correct response, he will simply continue to shift shields.

As the Elitist absorbs both verbal and physical, emotional and rational information the same way as the Feeler, the Driver, and the Analyzer, but in alternating sequences, he lags about fifteen seconds behind you as he reviews and sorts out what he has seen and heard. He is alternately attacking and defending. This frequently causes confusion and he lapses into Depression.

### STEP 8: "NOW I KNOW EXACTLY WHAT YOU MEAN": APPRECIATE THE IMPORTANCE OF TUNING IN ON EACH OTHER'S MOOD FREQUENCY

Now that you both see how the very meaning of what you say to each other in rejection becomes greatly distorted through no fault of your own, you should discuss the importance of tuning in on each other's Mood Frequency.

Given that only certain specific portions of what you say to each other actually penetrate each of your Dominant Mood shields, it stands to reason that if each of you communicates all (or at least most) of your meaning in terms of those specific portions, all (or most) of what you say to each other *will* get through. You will lessen the distortion effect on your meaning.

You will no longer be two people who constantly have their

wires of communication crossed, each hearing some garbled version of what is being said and erroneously assuming that what you hear *in your own terms* is what the other person is actually saying and really means.

You will be two people who genuinely want to get through to each other, each as sincerely intent on understanding the other person as you are on being understood yourself.

Discuss together how you can make the lines of communication between you as open, sharp, and crystal clear as possible.

Since your partner is not yet familiar with the techniques for tuning in on *your* Mood Frequency, we suggest that you first talk about their Mood Frequency exclusively, leaving your own till later (see pp. 150–155).

Outline how you have been using their Mood Frequency. They will undoubtedly have realized by now that you have been approaching them differently from the way you usually do. Or at very least, like the child who one day abruptly comes out of adolescence to discover with surprise that his parents seem suddenly to have become far more intelligent and understanding than they have been for the last seven or eight years, they will regard you with new respect.

Go over the techniques for Tuning In on Each Other's Mood Frequency, which you have been using point by point, encouraging them to offer suggestions that may vary any of these rules to better satisfy their particular needs.

Listen carefully to what they tell you, and pay particular attention to any suggestion that may come out in an evasive, faltering, or roundabout way. This faltering way of telling you how they want to be reached usually indicates that even though they may want you to know they have a deeply buried need, they are uncomfortable about telling you directly what it really is. Using their Mood Language, press them gently until you understand *exactly* what they are trying to tell you.

Leon and Marcie

The following story is a strikingly clear example of this type of need being brought out into the open between two people. It illustrates the power the *3Rs* has in bringing back together people who desperately need each other.

Leon is a fraud investigator from the West Coast who has been married for fifteen years and is the father of two children, aged twelve and nine. His marriage had deteriorated badly in the last five years, was "as strained as it could get," and had reached the point where his wife, Marcie, wanted a separation.

However, Leon, being a Driver, found it very difficult to face the idea that he had somehow not succeeded with his marriage, and was very reluctant just to give up on it and walk away without one final attempt at saving it.

Or what was left of it.

As a fraud investigator for an insurance company, Leon had attended several of Glenn Foster's seminars on crime-related interview methods and had a high regard for their practical usefulness.

When he heard that the techniques were being adapted to the area of relationships, he was hesitant about asking to try out the *3Rs*. But in the forlorn hope that it might offer something workable he could use to save his marriage, or at least understand where it had gone wrong, Leon determined to learn all he could.

During the *Read* stage, Leon immediately identified his wife Marcie as a Feeler and himself as a Driver. He realized she was not an off-key version of himself who could be understood only in his terms, but a highly individual, separate person, who not only did things differently but *thought* about things differently from the way he did. He began to see her as someone who could only be really understood in the context of her terms—not just his.

He began to see her, perhaps for the first time in their married life, not just as an extension of him but as a separate, unique, totally singular "person."

Long before Leon had even completed the *Respond* stage of the *3Rs,* he had come to the realization of how and why their different Driver and Feeler ways of doing things had been clashing so badly in rejection. He realized how the things they had once loved about each other now seemed to be the very things that frustrated and irritated both of them, alienating each from the other.

He determined to bring Marcie back into Acceptance.

Leon immediately began tuning in on Marcie's Mood Frequency, and that, to his mind, was the breakthrough. He was amazed that Marcie, after eighteen months of avoiding his company and hardly speaking to him, now suddenly seemed happy to be in his presence and carry on a conversation with him again.

However, Marcie still seemed to retain a deep, residual anger and resentment over Leon's past failings—or so Leon thought. He followed the rules on how to deal with the Mood of Anger, but every time she came out of that mood she would lapse into the Mood of Depression. Try as he might, Leon still seemed unable to isolate her theme and get at the root cause of her depression. He began to have the niggling feeling she was purposely keeping something from him— something she had never, in all their fifteen years together, trusted him to understand.

Nevertheless, sensing she was now in Acceptance of him again, he pressed on into the *Reciprocation* stage, and together they explored their differences. They actually reached the point where they could laugh over how blatantly their clashing had set up a predictable pattern of escalating conflict.

Leon came to see just how deeply his Driver's use of Anger and even Indignation alienated Marcie. She felt so threatened by his "overreactions to nothing" that she would do anything to avoid a direct confrontation. When she realized his dramatic reactions were just his way of expressing himself, and were not intended as personal assaults on her, Marcie's dread of bringing up anything that would set him off vanished, and she started to be even more forthcoming and open with him.

He realized that over the years she had come to see him as nothing more than a "control freak" who never bothered to listen to anything she said—so eventually she had simply stopped saying anything. Now that he was actually listening to what she said, and not interrupting or hurrying her to finish up, he realized that what she wanted to say in her own way was just as important as what he wanted to say. And he realized for the first time that her ideas were at least as mature, carefully considered, and "right" as his own.

When they reached the stage in *Reciprocation* where they began to discuss how to tune in on each other's Mood Frequency, Marcie began to understand the effort Leon had been putting in to try to understand who she was in her own right by carefully tuning in on *her* frequency (at the expense of his own), and she finally believed that he loved and appreciated her for who she was.

In return, she took the first step toward trusting him completely.

As they were discussing her Mood Language and how else he should approach her to really get through to Marcie in her terms and on her frequency, Leon kept sensing she wanted to tell him something specific but was holding back. He pressed her gently.

Suddenly it all came out in a rush: She had been repeatedly molested as a child and had never told a living soul. In the last five years she had been unable to cope with the shame of her secret and her life began falling apart.

Not trusting her husband to understand who she really was beneath the facade, she had closed herself off from him, and her resentment of him began to seethe. His "fiercely controlling protectiveness," which had given her such a warm sense of safety and security in the early years of their marriage, had begun instead to feel more like the dominating aggression she had fallen prey to as a child. She blamed Leon for making her feel like a victim yet again, this time as a grown woman. She blamed him for her inability to assert herself. She blamed him for making her deal with her misery in isolation.

She felt lost, lonely, and desperately alone in her marriage.

Finally, after weeks of slowly nurturing her trust, Leon had brought her to a point where Marcie believed he loved her for who she really was. She felt that if she did reveal her secret, he would not only *not* reject her but would even be able to *understand* her pain in her terms.

They said they clung to each other for hours that night. The intense loneliness each of them had been feeling vanished. It was replaced by a profound sense of shared need and trust.

## Our Secret Inadequacy: The Hidden Message of Our Theme

This is a clear, if dramatic, illustration of what can happen between two people when they use the *3Rs*. We all have some deeply hidden pain of a past failure or inadequacy that haunts us, despite our attempts to come to terms with it rationally.

It may be that we feel we were rejected by a parent in favor of a sibling; it may be that we once did something unforgivably venal and cruel to someone who did not deserve it; or perhaps we just feel we are not as intelligent or as sincere as we pretend to be.

Whatever it is, this secret motivates much of our behavior and is as important to us in our lives as Marcie's secret pain was in her life.

Whatever it is, this deep insecurity or inadequacy is always contained in our *theme.* Despite ourselves, it affects our attitudes and always leaks through into our Mood Language. We would all love to be able to share this hidden ache with someone who could understand what it means to us, someone who would not think any the less of us by knowing about it, someone who would be able to help us see it in perspective and might even love us for the way we have been dealing with it alone, locked up and hurting.

Find this pain in each other; share it; and relieve each other's shame.


## STEP 9: REACHING MUTUAL UNDERSTANDING

Both you and the person you love should now realize that the way each of you not only views your world, *but actually sees and hears it,* is very dissimilar. While neither of you can ever put yourself in the other's place and truly comprehend the view from there, you can now understand what that perspective must be like.

You are in a position not only to appreciate and respect but also finally to *understand* the differences between you.

Once you are in Mutual Acceptance and you both enjoy the way your differences counterbalance and complement each other, you both take pleasure in the fullness of a mutually supported and truly interdependent relationship.

However, with the onset of rejection, each of you withdraws into a private, self-centered inner core, and the very differences that once supported your togetherness now become barriers against it, *unless each of you knows how to get through those barriers.*

This is when it is of paramount importance to remember: (1.) how to deal with each other's Moods of Rejection; and (2.) how to tune in on each other's Mood Frequency.

When you have both reached this point in *Reciprocation,* you have already reached mutual understanding—which is the goal of the *3Rs.*

## The "Three Whites of the Eyes"

The eyes are said to be the windows of the soul. In one extreme case they are—very clearly.

The eyes of a person in great spiritual distress or torment will often display an unnatural rim of white between the lower lid and the iris, so that their eyes, when looking directly ahead, will have white showing not only on either side of the iris but also below it.

President John F. Kennedy displayed this phenomenon clearly during his televised address to the nation in October 1962 at the height of global tension over the Cuban missile crisis.

Although the strain on his face and in his voice told of the immense political and diplomatic pressure he was under to resolve the crisis in the West's favor, the "three whites" of his eyes revealed the terrible moral and spiritual angst he was enduring personally at the thought of being responsible for a possible nuclear holocaust.

When the crisis was over, Kennedy's eyes resumed their normal appearance.

The convicted 1960s California murderer and cult leader Charles Manson is so emotionally and spiritually disturbed he displays the "three whites" of his eyes permanently.

Although there are a few medical conditions (for example, hyperthyroidism) that cause this effect, it is generally only seen in someone who is highly stressed and who is attempting to cope with some terrible mental and emotional struggle.

If, during the stress of a difficult period in a relationship, your partner suddenly begins to show "three whites" in their eyes, forget your own problems. Your partner requires all the sympathetic understanding you are capable of offering.

THIRTEEN

# Differences: The Most Valuable Assets of Any Relationship

## THE *3Rs:* COMING TO CONCLUSIONS

The most usual—and most tragic—postmortem result of any failed or dying human relationship is to say that it failed or died because of the irreconcilable differences between the parties. As if, somehow, to be different from one's partner in a relationship was from the very beginning wrong.

Yet, all life and love can only thrive and grow because of difference. Sameness stultifies. Difference entices us with its promise of surprise, stimulation, new awareness, and wider understanding. Sameness only dulls.

To be fulfilled in a relationship does not involve hoping the other partner will eventually turn out to be the same as we are. To be fulfilled is to hope that the partner will be different, and that our combined differences will create a vital unity that will ultimately prove more exciting and satisfying than its individual parts.

Sadly, those differences between two separate and highly individual people—which originally are the source of such mutually attracting appeal, yield so much delight in their

discovery, confer so much warmth and comfort in their complementary wholeness, and such strength in their reconciliation—come to be blamed for the destruction of the relationship.

Somewhere along the line, the differences stopped being
accepted, wondered at, appreciated, and loved. They stopped
being seen as complementary and mutually strengthening.
They began instead to be taken for granted, and seen as
contrariness and attempts to be contradictory. They began to
grate. The more they clashed, the more incompatible became
those two separate and highly individual people who once
shared a mutually fulfilling relationship.

It is often said with regret that one's initial expectations in
a relationship are so high as to be unrealistic. They *are* unrealistic if one is not prepared to work to make those expectations come true, as one would be prepared to work in any
other similar choice—such as a career—to make expectations
come true.

*"Differences" are not what break a relationship. What
breaks up a relationship is refusing to accept that there are
differences and that they are in fact the finest assets of that relationship.*

The entire framework of the world is built on differences.
It is the merging of thesis and antithesis that brings into life
the synthesis of the whole.

To claim that the different is somehow unnatural is like
trying to create clones of oneself: exact mirror images. To
force other people to behave like us is merely to alienate
them because *they are not like us.* The irreconcilable differences so often are not irreconcilable at all: they are shallow
and self-serving expectations of sameness, which cannot be
reconciled with reality.

The real cause of the breakdown of love is a selfish desire
not to understand the differences in others, and by tyranny or
manipulation to try to force them to behave like us.

As we have seen, there is not one single personality type in the world but four. To force one to behave exactly the same way as another is as logically absurd as asking a cat to behave like a dog.

It is a case, put brutally, of like it or lump it. We can either view these differences as sources of wonder, nourishment, and comfort, or as irritations, causes for anger and withdrawal.

## THE 3Rs: MAKING THINGS WORK

In any relationship we should not be like Anne Tyler's "Accidental Tourist," but visitors who have carefully studied the ways and customs of those foreigners (the other personality types) and come to them ready, not to force them to do things the way we do them "back home," but to learn from them, and perhaps find out that sometimes they do things better than we do.

And they, in turn, may be surprised and charmed by some of our ways.

Just as an open-minded intertwining of different cultures can create a rich fabric of diversity, which strengthens and revitalizes each part, so the coming together of two personalities with their different ways of thinking and feeling, of doing and saying things, of living and even loving, can create an exquisite mosaic of love.

But we so seldom succeed because we are not prepared for it.

We would never arrive in an alien culture, with an unknown language and unfamiliar customs, without at least a guidebook or an elementary knowledge of how to deal with their strange differences. Yet we constantly leap into relationships without any plans whatsoever, merely hoping that "something will turn up" to make everything all right.

Without knowledge, foresight, and planning, nothing will

turn up. Without a thorough understanding of the *3Rs,* nothing—not pious hopes, or marriage counselors, or sympathetic friends—will make everything "all right."

We must: **read** in order to understand *who* other people are, *why* they think and feel the way they do, and *how* they convey what they think and feel; and understand the *real meaning* of what they are communicating in their terms by:

- recognizing and identifying their personality type; and
- observing and understanding how they use the Moods of Rejection to express their personality and communicate their needs.

So that we can then **respond** directly to *who* other people are, and *what* they are thinking and feeling; and understand and address their *real meaning* in their terms by:

- recognizing and identifying our own personality type,
- being aware that who we think we are is not what they think we are,
- using *their* Mood Frequency to communicate with them and satisfy their needs.

This then enables that other person to **reciprocate,** to read and understand *who* we are, *why* we think and feel the way we do, *how* we convey what we think and feel; and to respond to and address the *real meaning* of our Mood Frequency, in order to satisfy our needs in our own terms by:

- explaining how we recognize and understand the way they think, feel, and communicate their real meaning,
- comparing and contrasting, together, the different ways we both think, feel, and communicate our real meaning,

- discovering together how, and when, those differences both attract and repel, and
- *rediscovering and deepening our understanding of why our differences are so vital to a mutually fulfilling relationship.*

And, most important, if we are ever to satisfy that basic human need to share our hopes, dreams, and fears in the spirit of real love, we must learn to *Tune In to the Other Person's Mood Frequency.*

For the *Feeler,* by

- talking to them in terms of feelings
- being sensitive to their physical reactions
- being gentle, polite, and empathetic
- lowering our voice and slowing our speech
- presenting one idea at a time
- never dominating, controlling, or forcing them into anything
- being patient and never rushing them or interrupting their pauses or silences
- asking them directly what they think
- above all, *listening* when they talk

For the *Driver,* by

- being wholehearted in everything we say and do
- speeding up our thought processes and speaking more quickly
- speaking in concrete, not abstract, terms and always using examples from real situations to prove our point or back up our opinion
- being direct, succinct, and making our points quickly and without long-windedness
- being assertive, not backing down or giving in

- allowing them to control the direction and flow of any conversation (unless we are very sure we will win a continuous battle for domination)

For the *Analyzer,* by

- being calm and composed, mentally, emotionally, and physically
- concentrating our mental abilities and thinking clearly and logically
- always presenting our ideas precisely and succinctly in the form of facts that are either for or against them
- organizing and structuring our thoughts so as to be focused and directed when talking
- never speaking in emotive terms or showing our feelings
- always avoiding passing judgment or seeming to criticize them
- never confronting or dominating them, or trying to take control

For the *Elitist,* by

- always treating them with respect and due deference
- never trying to dominate or control them
- always staying clear-thinking and focused when talking to them on any subject
- concentrating on the "big picture" rather than minor details
- seeing this big picture from every perspective possible: intellectual and emotional, theoretical and practical, personal and impersonal
- never being impolite, crass, ill-mannered, or ill-bred
- always sympathetically bonding with their Depression.

### An Invitation to the Reader

Unlike many so-called self-help books that promise so much and deliver so little, *How Can I Get Through to You?* outlines a practical way of finding, deepening, and healing relationships that actually *works*.

*How Can I Get Through to You?* changes lives.

For possible inclusion in follow-up books in this series, the authors invite readers who have stories about how this book has made significant changes in *their* lives to write to:

> D. Glenn Foster and Mary Marshall
> ℅ Hyperion Publishers
> 114 Fifth Avenue
> New York, NY 10011

Anonymity, if requested, is guaranteed.

# APPENDIX: *THE LANGUAGE OF MOODS*

The verbal and non-verbal expressions of the Moods of Anger, Depression, Bargaining, and Denial, and how they are used in conflict to deflect, manipulate, and control others.

## ANGER

*Emotions Involved:* Frustration, disgust, indignance, annoyance, anxiety, vengeance

USED TO:
- Fight rejection
- Relieve built-up stress or frustration through venting
- Deflect and project responsibility from self to others
- Maintain control over the ebb and flow of information
- Control, dominate, and manipulate the other person
- Attack the other person's weakness of logic and emotion
- Cause stress in the other person
- Block being affected by the other person's emotions
- Force an issue

NOTE: Anger is the mood most often faked because it is the most effective in throwing off the other person.

227

*The Mood Language of the* Body *in Anger*

*Breathing:* Rate and depth of breathing increase and become more
   emphasized
   Breathing may even stop for short periods

*Skin coloring:* Reddens in blotches and becomes "purple with
   rage" in uncontrolled Anger—as the subcutaneous capillaries
   in the face and neck expand
   Pales and becomes chalky in controlled anger—as the capillaries
   close off

*Posture and muscle tone:* Becomes more erect as spinal muscles
   tighten
   Larger muscle groups flex as blood is rerouted through the body
   into these more powerful groups
   One or both shoulders rise to highest position
   "Jerking" movements begin

*Proxemics:* In red-hot Anger: increased use of intimate zone, or
   rapid movement from zone to zone
   In white-cold Anger: use of social or public zones only

*Eyes:* Become bright and hard
   Stare coldly and defiantly
   Try to "stare down" an opponent—to dominate and control, or
   Glare almost without blinking—to manipulate
   Stare coldly with a false look of happiness frozen on the face
   Muscles tense around the eyes
   Muscle tics may begin at the side of one or both eyes—to hold
   Anger in check
   Upper and lower eyelids may narrow into a squint
   White may become visible below irises (see Box, p. 219)

*Eyebrows:* Come together and close down toward eyes in a frown,
   or
   Pull up, exaggerating the size of glaring eyes

*Forehead:* Vertical furrows form as the eyebrows come together, or
   Horizontal furrows form as the eyebrows rise
   Pulse may start throbbing at temples

*Mouth:* Lips tighten: either drawn back or pursed together
   Lip or tongue biting may begin—to control Anger
   Teeth clench or grind

*Nose:* Nostrils dilate and may flare
   Rapid, audible inhalation and exhalation through nose begins

*Head:* Jaw juts out and head goes back without a side tilt
  Jaw muscles tighten and may throb
  Head turns away as large breath of air is inhaled loudly
  "Figure L" may form with thumb placed below chin and index
    finger extended up to the side of the temple

*Arms:* Come in close to the body
  Cross very high over the chest, with shoulders raised, with or
    without the accompanying formation of a fist

*Hands:* Point or shake in other person's body space
  Pound, slam, or drum on inanimate objects
  Fists form, either in plain sight or hidden
  Hands go to hips, elbows out. In males, fingers may point toward
    genital area in classic anger/aggression/domination pose
  Hand begins to rub back of neck—may be prelude to violent re-
    action
  Hands "steeple" together in a prayer position—to show contempt
    for other person

*Legs:* Form "figure 4" with ankle of one leg resting on knee of
    other leg—to hold other person off
  One leg crosses over the other at the knee, with the lower part of
    the upper leg swinging rapidly back and forth—in females espe-
    cially, a sign of growing Anger
  Legs and knees begin to shake

*Feet:* Heels come together with toes pointed outward in a cocky "V"
    (military position)
  Foot begins to tap—to show agitation or impatience

### The Mood Language of the Voice in Anger

*Speech mannerisms:* In red-hot (uncontrolled) Anger: verbal attacks
    begin to spew out at rapid-fire speed, together with jumping
    from subject to subject before completion of sentences, trip-
    ping over words, spluttering, and emitting sounds that are not
    words—because of the speeding up of thought processes
  In white-cold (controlled) Anger: speech begins to slow down
    considerably as a basic, succinct vocabulary is used with all syl-
    lables stressed in a clear, cold tone of delivery—as the need to
    control the other person grows

*Tone:* Threatening, sarcastic, mocking, bombastic, authoritarian,
    callous

*Rate:* In red-hot Anger: increases
  In white-cold Anger: decreases

*Volume:* In red-hot Anger: increases for stress and emphasis
  In white-cold Anger: decreases for stress and emphasis

*Pitch:* Rises because of internal stress (throat is sometimes cleared
    to re-set pitch)

*What is said:* Anything to attack other people: who they are, what
    they stand for, their logic, their emotions, their values, their po-
    sition
  *Anything* anyone says is attacked
  Trivial, irrelevant details are latched onto and argued about


## DEPRESSION

*Emotions Involved:* Sadness, anxiety, self-pity, self-disgust, fear, re-
    gret, anguish

USED TO:
  • Flee rejection
  • Attack self
  • Protect self from further attack from others (closure)
  • Soothe and comfort self
  • Excuse self for being unable to do anything to correct the situ-
    ation
  • Elicit sympathy and manipulate the other person into bonding
  • Express the pain being experienced


### The Mood Language of the Body in Depression

*Breathing:* Becomes deeper and slower and more exaggerated—to
    communicate the depression

*Posture:* Becomes slouched and slumped. Movements become slow
    and lethargic

*Muscle tone:* Becomes almost nonexistent

*Proxemics:* Decreases distance to intimate or personal zone when
    trying to bond
  Increases distance to social or public zone when wanting to be
  alone

*Eyes:* Become dull and lackluster
  Eye contact becomes less and less frequent

Normal blink rate becomes disrupted
Exaggerated crying may begin

*Eyebrows:* Lower

*Forehead:* Three to five deep horizontal furrows form

*Mouth:* Lips slacken, corners may turn down
May begin to quiver—to control crying or as a prelude to crying

*Head:* Chin lowers
Hand to head gestures begin to increase, especially any rubbing of the head
Frequently, head is placed in hands

*Hands:* Rub together
Rub at inside of the thighs—to comfort self
Frequently touch the face, rub at or cover eyes, cover mouth, massage sides of face or head, hold head
In extreme Depression, may form a "suicide finger" gesture (index finger extending and touching at the temple, hand curled back in "pistol" representation).

### The Mood Language of the Voice in Depression

*Speech mannerisms:* Delivery becomes halting; sentences are broken, then restarted from the beginning or from the middle; thoughts are repeated or trail off; logic is interrupted
There is a great deal of pausing and hesitation
As Depression locks in, difficulty in understanding what the other person is saying. Confusion, distortion, misinterpretation, and often complete incomprehension of entire blocks of a conversation

*Tone:* Self-pitying, sarcastic, and belittling toward self, aggrieved, pained

*Pitch, rate, and volume:* Decrease when "experiencing" own pain
Increase when trying to communicate pain and bond

*What is said:* Anything to attack themselves:
How much this conflict is costing them personally, how deeply it is affecting them
Expressions of regret over the past and gloomy predictions about the future
How other person's remarks are tearing them to pieces

How they are not sleeping and/or eating properly anymore
How their health has been affected by continuing conflict

## BARGAINING

*Emotions Involved:* Fear, anxiety, panic

USED TO:
- Both fight and flee rejection
- Deactivate conflict
- Cut deal for self
- Deflect and prevent a head-on attack
- Undermine and interrupt the flow of rejection
- Shield own Denial and camouflage own Anger
- Simulate false Acceptance and place self in mock subservient/submissive position
- Manipulate
- Appease the other person by making his/her needs paramount
- Create trust and force a bond
- Persuade the other person to see the unfairness of the situation

### *The Mood Language of the* Body *in Bargaining*

*Breathing:* Rate increases slightly

*Posture:* Becomes supplicative, cajoling
  Submission postures appear—in the hope that they will be "contagious"

*Proxemics:* Normally moves into intimate or personal zones

*Eyes:* Eye contact becomes excessive
  Eyes express sincerity—which may or may not be genuine
  May glance to ceiling to imply, "you've got to believe me, I'm helpless in this situation"
  Inappropriate crying may begin—to manipulate further

*Eyebrows:* Become expressive—to accentuate manipulation

*Mouth:* Frequent smiling begins—usually only upper teeth shown (not genuine)
  A rapid series of smiles may be used to manipulate
  Smile will stay on face longer if it has the desired effect

*Head:* Tilts to one side—to show interest in what is being said

*Hands:* One or both hands raise in helpless or hopeless gesture
Palms frequently open outward
Palms turn toward other person as hair is flicked back (in females, used as a flirtation signal)

*Feet:* Turn in toward each other at the toes with the head slightly tilted to one side—to show sexual interest

### The Mood Language of the Voice in Bargaining

*Speech mannerisms:* Everything said in an "over-nice" manner: polite, gracious, solicitous, kind, considerate, gentle
Often said in a flattering and/or flirtatious way
Delivery often accompanied by a great deal of false laughter and excessive smiling

*Tone:* Cajoling, wheedling, conciliatory, sincere, trusting, nonthreatening

*Pitch:* Down

*Volume:* Low and controlled

*Rate:* Slowed for emphasis, or
Speeded up for mock enthusiasm

*What is said:* Anything that emphasizes and upgrades the other person's importance and deemphasizes and downgrades one's own
Addresses the other person in laudatory terms with frequent use of pet names or full titles
Anything that wards off an attack: illnesses or not feeling well, medical treatments, nervous conditions, high blood pressure
Religious, moral, or ethical piety, including complimentary statements made about other person by others
Anything that wins the other person over: addressing another person's problems before one's own, seeing other's point of view and conceding small points; making promises about what will happen in the future (often will use "carrots" such as the presentation of a gift, or the promise of a purchase of a gift in the future)
Anything flattering and or flirtatious

## DENIAL

NOTE: There are two forms of Denial:
  (1) Denial of the truth to self or self-deception;
  (2) Denial of the truth to others or lying

*Emotions Involved:* Fear, anxiety, anger, disgust, contempt, suspicion, doubt

USED TO:
  • Flee rejection
  • Block or contradict reality
  • Ignore a threatening situation, issue, or personality
  • Prevent an objective view of the truth
  • Protect self by blocking the effect of unpleasant emotions and thoughts
  • Deliver a lie either to self or to others
  • Justify refusal to accept any other position
  • Gain acceptance by trying to convince others theirs is the only way to see things
  • Buy time when confronted with the truth
  • Support all other Moods of Rejection, and control other forms of manipulation

Denial in Form 1 shows fewer readable signals, because it is more controlled and there is less stress when it is challenged.

Denial in Form 2 shows more readable signals, because it is less controlled and there is a great deal of stress when the lie is challenged.

### *The Mood Language of the* Body *in Denial When That Denial Is Confronted or Challenged*

*Breathing:* Increases in Form 1
  Appears normal in Form 2
  A quick, sudden intake of air—shock or surprise when confronted

*Posture and muscle tone:* Body turns or begins to lean away when confronted
  Rigid, "uptight" movements suddenly appear, then, as confrontation increases, become excessive (these movements are less obvious and more controlled in Form 2)

*Proxemics:* Tends to use outer zones in Form 1
  Tends to use closer zones in Form 2—for control and emphasis

*Eyes:* Begin to take on an overall worried look—because their reality is not being accepted

Eye contact becomes more prolonged—to attempt to communicate by "an honest look" that what is being said is true; or

Eye contact breaks frequently for other matters: readjusting clothing or jewelry, winding watch; picking hair or lint off clothing or furniture; cleaning or adjusting eyeglasses. In fact, anything to avoid facing the issue head-on

Pupils constrict

Normal rate of blinking increases

*Mouth:* Tightens. Lips are clamped shut when not speaking

The hand goes up to cover the mouth at the same time as there is an impediment of speech

*Eyebrows:* In Form 1, Denial of the truth to self, one eyebrow may rise while the other remains stationary—indicating denial and suspicion of an issue, and tremendous doubt and suspicion at what the other person is saying

Both eyebrows rise—indicating shock at being caught "off-balance"

*Nose:* Touching at the bottom part of the nose with thumb and forefinger to ease tingling "Pinocchio Syndrome" sensation—an admission of belief that their position could be wrong but that they still intend to maintain at least the appearance of Denial (see p. 69)

*Head:* Frequently supported in the hands

Touching at the face increases, especially in an area between the roots of the lower teeth and the center of the nose, with concentration at the sides of the mouth

*Arms:* Come in close to the body—for protection of the torso

*Hands:* One hand may be thrown away from the body—to dismiss an idea, concept, or question (normally seen in Form 1)

One or both hands, palms upward, raised toward the ceiling or sky—to harden up and emphasize a point they themselves do not believe in, often accompanied by exhalation of a deep breath as both an indication of contempt and a stalling tactic

*Legs:* Start crossing and uncrossing when confronted in Form 1—to stall, buy time, and dissipate built-up energy

One leg stretched out straight in front of the other when sitting

*The Mood Language of the* Voice *in Denial When That Denial
Is Confronted or Challenged:*

*Speech mannerisms:*
  *Speech disturbances appear*
     Slurring of words—when their thought line is not well pre-
        pared in Form 1
     Stuttering and stammering; use of "ah," "er," "um," and "uh";
        grunts and sounds from lips that are not words—used to stall
        and buy time to think in both forms
     Sudden dropping of suffixes on words: -ly, -ing, -ed
  *Language fluency begins to break down*
     Sudden correction of a sentence without prompting, and repeti-
        tion of the information in this sentence several times—when
        they feel they have said too much or too little in Form 2
     Speaking in incomplete sentences, restarting sentences in the
        middle, skipping around in sentences—when they see other
        person is not being taken in by their Denial in Forms 1 and 2
     Clipping of word endings, cutting words in half or omitting
        words—when they want to say as little as possible and to con-
        trol what is being said in Forms 1 and 2
     Pronoun shifting: from singular to plural, plural to singular
        when in high stress in Forms 1 and 2
  *Mental blocks begin to appear*
     Sudden inability to recall things: "I can't remember," "I don't
        think so," "Not that I can think of," "Not that I can totally re-
        call"—as selective recall gives them time to get their story
        (alibi) straight, on *initial* confrontation in Forms 1 and 2
  *Vocabulary suddenly expands and certain words and expressions
  start being used*
     Vocabulary range expands to include use of words, phrases,
        sentences, or quotations that they normally do not use—to
        make their version of the truth more believable in Form 2
     Words like "really," "generally," "usually," "almost," "hardly,"
        "hardly ever," start being used for the first time—to equivo-
        cate their denial
     Expressions they actually mean the opposite of begin to be
        used: "To tell the truth," "to be a hundred percent honest,"
        "truthfully speaking," "talking openly," "being straightfor-
        ward," "to open up," "frankly" in Form 2
     Oaths, or requests that drastic things happen to loved ones or
        themselves begin to be expressed: "May God strike me
        dead"—to prove their point

Third-person words begin to appear: "others," "they," "them," "everybody," "nobody"—as an appeal to universal acknowledgment to prove their version of the truth, and to remove self from involvement in blame, in Forms 1 and 2

*Normal conversational flow suddenly becomes disrupted*

Interruption of other person's comments or questions—as they do not want to hear the other person's version of reality or face that person's reaction to their Denial in Form 1

Restating of questions put to them, answering of a question with another question, rewording of the question put to them and asking it of the other person, pretending the question was not understood, asking for the question to be repeated—to stall and buy time in Forms 1 and 2

*Rate:* Slowed when weighing content in Forms 1 and 2

In Form 2, speeded up at point when rehearsed and well-thought-out lie is reached—to get all the information out

*Volume:* Up slightly in Form 1

Down slightly in Form 2

*Pitch:* Up—in protest, more so in Form 1 than in Form 2

*What is said:* Anything that will convince the other person they have no reason to lie, either to self or others:

Proclamations of honesty, integrity, frankness, religiousness begin to be made

A great deal of information about what they have *not* done or are *not* going to do is divulged voluntarily

Disparaging remarks about others become frequent

Descriptions of people, places, things, or reasons are given in negative rather than positive terms

Anything being discussed becomes more and more based in emotionality rather than factual reasoning

The author wishes to acknowledge the following sources used in this book.

*Barbara Walters: An Unauthorized Biography,* Jerry Op-
penheimer (St. Martin's Press, 1990), p. 114.

*From Where I Sit: Merv Griffin's Book of People,* with
Peter Barsocchini (Pinnacle Books, 1982), p. 198.

*The Great TV Sitcom Book,* Rick Mitz (Richard Marek
Publishers, 1980), pp. 262 and 263.

"Hugh and Barbara Talk About Each Other!" an article
by Alan Ebert in *Good Housekeeping,* January 1992.

"Kissinger" an article in the *New Republic* by Oriana
Fallaci, December 16, 1975.

*Kissinger,* Marvin Kalb and Bernard Kalb (Little, Brown
and Company, 1974), pp. 11 and 12.

*Kissinger: A Biography,* Walter Isaacson (Simon and
Schuster, 1992).

*Murphy Brown, Anatomy of a Sitcom,* Robert S. Alley
and Irby B. Brown (Delta, 1990), pp. 248 and 249.

"A President-Elect Who Has a Winning Way with People," *The New York Times,* November 4, 1992.

## ABOUT THE AUTHORS

D. Glenn Foster is a well-known interview consultant who instructs the FBI, the U.S. State Department, and the Federal Bureau of Alcohol, Tobacco, and Firearms in professional interview techniques. He also has lectured to professional bodies of judges, trial attorneys, psychiatrists, and psychologists. The originator of the Foster Method—which is in constant use professionally and is now adapted for mainstream use—he is in demand by federal, state, and local agencies to conduct interviews in major criminal and civil cases throughout the United States. He lives in Atlanta.

Mary Marshall is an attorney with an extensive background in family and matrimonial law. She has been instrumental in broadening the Foster Method into the field of interpersonal relations and is currently working on its application in situations of domestic violence and how people deceive each other. She lives in Barto, Pennsylvania.

LaVergne, TN USA
08 August 2010
192419LV00004BA/12/A